July 18, 2002

TWO RELIGIONS-ONE CHURCH

Division and Destiny
In the Anglican Church of Canada

by

George R. Eves

Lorde we beseche thee, graunt thy people [illegible] the infeccions of the Deuil, and with [illegible] to folowe thee the onelye God; T[illegible] our Lorde.

(The Collect for *The xviii Sondaye* in the 154[illegible] Common Prayer)

Published by V.O.I.C.E. (Vocalizing Our Interest in Church Endeavours), 87 Carleton St., Saint John, New Brunswick, E2L 2Z2

ISBN # 0-9683030-0-5

COVER DESIGN and GRAPHICS by Billie Nodelman

TABLE OF CONTENTS

FOREWORD

The Most Reverend Harold L. Nutter, Archbishop (Ret.) of the Province of Canada and the Diocese of Fredericton.

It is customary for the writer of the "Foreword" to express thanks for the privilege of commending the book. While I do this gladly, I am also aware that the subject is both disturbing and challenging.

The Rev. George Eves has produced a work which will be seen as challenging and prophetic, or reactionary and ultra-conservative, depending on the preconceptions of the reader. It is just this possible diversity of readers' reaction which makes it an important statement of the contemporary reality in our Church.

I am certain that very few people will find comfort in the thesis of the writer. The title, "Two Religions - One Church" and the various chapter themes may appear to have prejudged the current situation of the Church, but the analysis of the factors contributing to that situation should challenge our Anglican people to consider the basis of their faith. This is focused for the reader in the argument that there are "two incompatible and competing religions within the Church", expressing themselves in the authority of experience (liberalism) versus the authority of Divine revelation (orthodoxy).

I share the author's conviction that we must face the question of our authority in the contemporary Church. The Church is not a democratic society but a theocracy, and God is its head, and not the Bishop or the Primate, or the Priest, or anyone else. Authority rests upon the revelation of God in Jesus Christ, and has not been delegated to the consensus which is arrived at so often today in meetings, whether it be of Bishops or Clergy or Synods. Consensus, a worthy goal in some contexts, can also simply be another means of having everybody decide what is the lowest common denominator. We have to realize that revelation is a given, and many of us in my generation tried to find a more acceptable and more relevant way.

Which brings us back to this book. The writer's assessment of the crisis in the Church is based on such factors as falling membership, decline in evangelistic mission, rejection of traditional worship, uncertain teaching, blurred lines of authority, and clerical elitism without proper accountability.

The author argues that the disagreement of those who see the relationship of homosexuals to the Church as a question of human/social justice and those who claim the authority of Scripture as a basis for their orthodox/traditional stand is the issue which will reveal the Church's division into "two incompatible and competing religions."

Readers will be challenged to think deeply about the ethical, cultural and theological ramifications of the issues and hopefully will wish to pursue the debate further.

Whether one agrees with the Rev. George Eves or not, I believe this work is one which deserves careful and prayerful study, and it may assist many of our people to reaffirm their faith, and pray God, it may point the Church itself to a renewal of its mission and its authority.

So the call is surely to return to the foundation truths, to the authority based on the revelation of God, to a worship which proclaims those truths and that authority. Then we need not fear. For thank God, when we do that it will cease to be my Church and become once again our Lord's Church. So we may confidently again be the living Body of Christ and show forth the wonder of His choice of His people and our oneness in Him.

ACKNOWLEDGMENTS

How many times has an author proclaimed how impossible it is to acknowledge all the persons who have made a contribution to his book. Well, you can add this one to the list! The reality is that so many have helped in so many different ways that any attempt to name them will fall short of the mark. However, this does not lessen the obligation to try. I apologize in advance to those who should be included here but are not. Those I have forgotten do thou O Lord remember.

To my wife Deborah and my daughters Rhiannon and Sarah I have to say, "Hi! Remember me?" For two years they have put up with the disappearing Dad. Their support has been unflagging and has been a constant source of encouragement. Much of my share of the household duties has fallen to my family. I guess I am going to have to resume my place in the order of things now that this task is done. Maybe I should write another...

Then again, maybe not! In the meantime I would like to acknowledge and thank the following persons (in no particular order): Allan and Douglas Silk, Billie Nodelman, Stan "There is Hope" Izon, Helen Ellis, Gwen MacKnight, Nessim and Laraine Isa, Frances Morrisey, Pat and Barb Loring, Byron Phillips, Jo Jones, Deborah Hughes, Gene and Bea Mealey, Sylvia Davidson, Bob and Barb Likely, Phyllis Ratcliffe, Keith and Carol Wilson, Kay Armstrong, Elsie Northrup and the Reverends John Pearce, Canon Stuart Allan, Canon Philip Ward, Dr. Tom Robinson, Eric Phinney, Keith Osborne, Anthony Bassett, Archdeacon Lyman Harding, Bruce McKenna, Archbishop Harold Nutter, Bishop George Lemmon, Greg McMullen, and Dr. J. I. Packer.

Special mention must go to Clifford Maude who has served as sounding-board, critic and supporter through countless conversations over even more countless cups of coffee. Also included in the category of "special mention" are the three persons who read the manuscript and helped make many many improvements: Leslie Allan, Rebecca Ellis and the Rev. Walter Vipperman.

My secretary, Melvina Vail, has, as usual, gone the second mile in carrying out the countless jobs I have asked her to do. Her competence, enthusiasm and support have been a real source of strength.

I would like to thank the Commonwealth and Continental Church Society in Halifax for its generous financial support as well.

Last but not least I wish to thank the congregation, vestry and wardens of St. John's (Stone) Church as well as all those who have kept this project in their prayers.

When you begin to put a list like this together you realize afresh how important it is to know that you are not alone. This has sustained me more than once when I felt overwhelmed by doubts and frustrations. Only in His Presence will we know the true dimensions of the struggle. I thank God for you all.

PREFACE

For I wrote you out of great distress and anguish of heart and with many tears, not to grieve you but to let you know the depth of my love for you.
(1 Corinthians 2:4)

I am an Anglican by choice. Like a significant proportion of Anglican clergy I came to faith in the bosom of another denomination. In my case it was Pentecostal and I have always been thankful to God for the faithful preaching of the Gospel that I was under for the first two decades of my life. However, after a crisis of faith I began to yearn for a church that had a deeper intellectual tradition while at the same time anchored in historic Christian faith and worship. When I discovered the Book of Common Prayer in the context of the evangelical Anglican community, I knew I was home. I have been a committed Anglican ever since and have been ordained for over fifteen years.

I feel it necessary to start this Preface on a personal note because what I have to say in this little book will inevitably be interpreted as an attack on the Anglican Church of Canada. In fact it is a wholly *defensive* action arising out of love and concern for the Church. When a man senses that his home is threatened he will do all that he can to preserve it. This is how I perceive my purpose. I am convinced that my spiritual home, the Anglican Church of Canada, is in a crisis of unprecedented proportions and that in order to find the way out it is necessary to have as accurate an understanding of that crisis as is possible. My hope is that this present effort will make a small contribution towards such an understanding. Even if my reasoning is rejected it can still help fulfill my purpose if counter-arguments are put forward which provide a more accurate picture. While I am currently convinced of the validity of my position, I hope I am open to change in the light of superior arguments or further evidence.

It is an overriding concern for my Church which compels me to undertake this project. However, there are at least three more reasons which have contributed to my decision to proceed. The first of these is personal. For some time I have felt the need to systematize my own scattered thoughts and articulate them in a way that made sense to me, first of all, and then to others as well. To do this I need to test fully my own positions. There is no better (or more intimidating) way in which to do this than by submitting them to public scrutiny. Secondly, I have been moved on many occasions by lay people who have confessed utter bewilderment as to what has happened to their Church. There is no short answer to this question! It is for them, especially, that I write. For a variety of reasons this will not necessarily be easy reading but I trust that they will persevere and receive some further understanding for their pains. Finally, some time ago I entered into correspondence with a colleague who had challenged some comments I had made in print on the subject of homosexuality. After several letters I finally realized that we seemed to be coming at this question from such different perspectives that I could not adequately express my position without trying to explain more fully why I was saying what I was saying and why I was continuously frustrated at our inability to connect. So, this is for him too. I will be sure to mail him a free copy!

In truth, however, these "reasons" are really only rationalizations. I think it was C. S. Lewis who likened the writing process to being "pregnant with book". This wonderful phrase perfectly describes how I have felt over the last twenty or so years. Some gestation period! As I write this I do not know if my child will be stillborn or robust, significant only to myself or able to make a worthwhile contribution to society. Whichever it is, like so many before me, I have no choice but to give birth and entrust the future to God.

I finish this with a quote from the Book of Common Prayer. It is part of the Bishop's Charge to those about to be ordained (p. 649). It is my hope that what I have done in this book might be taken as an attempt to be faithful to the high calling that has been put upon me as a priest in the Church of God.

> **Have always therefore printed in your remembrance, how great a treasure is committed to your charge. For they are the sheep of Christ, which he bought with his death, and for whom he shed his blood. The Church and Congregation whom you must serve, is his spouse and his body. And if it shall happen the same Church, or any member thereof, to take any hurt or hindrance by reason of your negligence, ye know the greatness of the punishment that will ensue. Wherefore consider with yourselves the end of your ministry towards the children of God, towards the spouse and body of Christ; and see that you never cease your labour, your care and diligence, until you have done all that lieth in you, according to your bounden duty, to bring all such as are or shall be committed to your charge, unto that agreement in the faith and knowledge of God, and to that ripeness and perfectness of age in Christ, that there be no place left among you, either for error in religion or for viciousness in life.**

George R. Eves
Saint John, New Brunswick
January, 1998

INTRODUCTION

He himself was not the light: he came only as a witness to the light. (John 1:8)

The Anglican Church of Canada is in a profound crisis of confusion and paralysis due to its unacknowledged and irreconcilable division into two incompatible religions. An alien and open-ended liberalism has grafted itself onto the original traditional/orthodox Christianity. Two different natures underlie these religions. Liberalism has no doctrinal centre and is thus forever fragmenting into newer configurations. Traditional/orthodox Christianity is committed to a foundation of doctrinal essentials which, in spite of considerable diversity, provides the basis for real unity. This fundamental duality has led to an unrelenting series of conflicts on a wide variety of issues over the last thirty or so years. It is here that we find the primary reason for the gridlock that often seems to afflict much of the Church's endeavours.

While the root of these struggles may remain largely unrecognized by many, the basic unresolved tension between the two religions is coming into clearer focus over the issue of homosexuality. Indeed, there are signs that if the denomination moves officially to accept homosexual practice, it will be torn apart along the fault lines where these two religions digress. Fortunately the House of Bishops has recently decided to continue its ban on the ordination of practicing homosexuals and the blessing of same-sex unions. This will probably prevent a plunge into the abyss for as long as the ban remains in effect and is supported by the General Synod. Ordinary Anglicans must write their members of General Synod in order to help ensure that this takes place. Hopefully sufficient time will then be won to allow the Church to confront the true dimensions of its crisis before it is too late.

As thousands of ordinary Anglicans become more directly involved in Church life a new institutional dynamic will be created. We face an unprecedented opportunity to discover together just what it is that forms the basic message and mission of our denomination. This must be done if we are to come to a common mind on the many issues that we encounter in a modern secular society. I will argue that ultimately the only way forward involves the re-affirmation of the traditional/orthodox faith of our Church's founders and the repudiation of liberalism. While no one relishes the prospect of developing an undoubtedly difficult and painful process whereby this might take place, such a route is infinitely preferable to the trauma of the abyss.

I shall attempt to give an account of how we got to this point in our history. This is not history as it is usually written with names, dates and places. Rather it is a kind of spiritual history, an internal history, a history of ideas. As such it is even more open to criticism and correction than is the normal sort of history. However that may be, it is necessary to make the attempt to understand. I am fortified by the fact that this is not a history confined entirely to the Anglican Church of Canada but is part of a pattern many commentators have observed in various so-called "mainline" denominations in North America.

In fact, others have applied a similar analysis in an attempt to throw some light on the malaise that is affecting the entire society. In this regard I refer the reader to the highly acclaimed *Culture Wars: The Struggle to Define America* by James Davidson Hunter which traces out the division in that country between those who continue to hold to absolute values and the liberal establishment which does not. He comes to conclusions similar to mine, only on a much wider scale. Along the same lines, the esteemed liberal social critic, Todd Gitlin, has reluctantly determined that the great liberal vision of encouraging diversity (which I characterize as "fragmentization") is unable to provide any "glue" to hold us all together. This is the major theme of his recent book, *Twilight of Common Dreams*. Thus my own analysis is both a conscious and unconscious following in the path of many others and this gives me courage to believe that it is not entirely eccentric or without merit.

I also take refuge in the fact that I am imitating the methodology of the sixteenth-century Anglican divine, Richard Hooker. He is generally acknowledged as the greatest of all Anglican theologians. It was his magisterial work, *The Laws of Ecclesiastical Polity* (1597), written against the Puritans on the one hand and the Roman Catholics on the other, which defined and established the renowned Anglican "middle way". He could only do this by applying unrelenting logic to the arguments of his opponents. At the beginning of a section dealing with the proper function of sermons he made the following comment:

> Our desire is in this present controversy, as in the rest, not to be carried up and down with the waves of uncertain arguments, but rather positively to lead on the minds of the simpler sort by plain and easy degrees, till the very nature of the thing itself do make manifest what is truth. (*Laws of Ecclesiastical Polity*, Book V, Ch. xxi, 2, Keble Edition, p. 84, Vol.2)

This is a wonderful articulation of what I am trying to do in this book. I wish to show forth the reality of our Church and its history for all to see. I do not do this as a voyeur but as a diagnostician. Like a woman examining herself for breast cancer I proceed with more than a little self-interest. Even the examination takes courage however. Discovering a lump is bad news, but not discovering it is even worse. Painful though it may be, such knowledge is the first step toward healing.

While the first five chapters of the book offer an analysis of our current crisis and attempt to explain how we got into it in the first place, the last five explore what is likely to happen in the future. I make no claim to be a prophet or the son of a prophet. The Bible itself has some dire warnings for those who presume to speak in the name of the Lord. It also indicates that a true prophet will be known by his track record. I have none beyond that of my service as a minister of the Gospel. However, some things are self-evident to anyone who cares to think at all about the situation in which we find ourselves. We are already divided in such a fundamental manner that there can be no serious question that this division will shape our destiny. Either the two religions will go their separate ways into schism (two denominations) or we will re-affirm the traditional/orthodox Christianity of our founders through a process of repentance and conversion. In this lies our hope. Our only hope.

Finally I would note that much to my surprise the nature of the book changed radically in the course of its writing. Never intended as a disinterested analysis, it has actually become part of an effort to give ordinary Anglicans a voice at this critical time in our history. As the reader will discover, the book itself is a key element in a wider proposal which may, under God, help bring renewal to the denomination. In this sense the book has taken on the characteristics of the "Tracts" which were written during the early years of the Anglo-Catholic revival in the last century. These were relatively short essays on serious theological questions and were printed up for individual circulation. They proved so successful that the whole movement took the name "Tractarian". Difficult as it may be for an evangelical Anglican to consider himself an heir to this part of our heritage, I do acknowledge the debt and admit the parallel! The Tractarians stirred things up marvelously and forced Anglicans of their day to consider again those things that were truly important. I would be more than proud to assume such a worthy mantle.

CHAPTER ONE

Fears and Fantasies

Dear friends, do not believe every spirit, but test the spirits, to see whether they are from God, because many false prophets have gone out into the world. (*1* John 4:1)

(i) Introduction: Natural Barriers

At first glance many Anglicans will automatically resist my thesis. Some will even be shocked and angered. They will see in this work an attack upon the Church and its leaders. Some will view what I have to say as an attempt to resurrect the "old" divisions that have plagued our church and which thankfully have fallen into irrelevance in recent years. Still others will sense that I am only making a bad situation worse by airing these things in public. While these reactions are certainly understandable I believe they are unfounded and based upon certain misunderstandings as to the nature of Anglicanism. While I naturally think that the main argument of the book will serve to dispel these "fears and fantasies", they also need to be addressed directly at this point in an attempt to clear some of the debris from the path for those who might hesitate to proceed further.

(ii) The Spirit of Intolerance?

First of all, there will be some, especially perhaps among our current leaders, who will feel that what I have to say will only be rubbing salt in the wounds that divide us. Why can't we just agree to disagree and tolerate one another's differences as members of the same family. Surely this is the Christian thing to do. While this is an attractive point of view for a number of reasons, it begs the question of truth by assuming that all points of view have a legitimate place on the Anglican spectrum. I hope to show, in fact, why it is partly because of this attitude that we have ended up in crisis. For those of us who insist that there is a right and a wrong such calls for undefined tolerance can only be taken as a way of silencing our voice right from the start.

On the other hand we are told that every voice is to be heard. If what I have to say fails to ring true or is even proven false by better arguments and/or evidence, then the Church will be all the stronger for it. Many of those who share my basic outlook will have to face the facts and change our views. In this way there will be greater unity among us. However, if both sides simply continue to drift apart in a silent, dangerous tolerance of each other, we have much to lose. As I am presently convinced that this is exactly what is happening, perhaps I will be forgiven for speaking out in this fashion.

(iii) The Ghost of Parties Past?

Secondly, it is often said, in Anglican contexts, that "Thank goodness the divisions that marked our past are now behind us." Am I not then merely returning to the "bad old days" by wanting to address the whole question of "division" once again? Surely this would be counter-productive at this stage in the Church's life. Strangely enough, I am in full-hearted accord with this sentiment! I have no desire whatever to conjure up our old "party spirits" which had us securely fixed in our various camps: "low-church/evangelical", "high-church/anglo-catholic" and "broad-church/moderate". These no longer exist as such. The old battles that were fought over what now appear to be trifling matters (e.g., the wearing of stoles or the use of mitres) have been largely relegated to the ash heap of history. This indeed is cause for rejoicing.

My point is that the current division in our denomination is of a wholly different order. It makes our previous differences look like a children's quarrel. Not only is our unity threatened but also our very existence. Whereas we used to be divided on what most saw as secondary matters, today we are divided on core issues. I hope to show that this is indeed the case and how it is that this has come about. Perhaps the serious nature of these allegations will encourage concerned Anglicans to read on.

(iv) A Rebellious Spirit?

(a) Authority Beyond Question?

Thirdly, and perhaps most importantly, there are many Anglicans who are extremely uncomfortable with any suggestion that officials who hold legitimate leadership positions in their Church could seriously be charged with coming to believe in a different "religion" than that of traditional/orthodox Christianity. Have they not been chosen by the Church? Are not most of them ordained? Are not some of them bishops? Surely it is vain to oppose this leadership. After all it *is* the leadership. Does not the Holy Spirit direct the whole process? Should we not stop our ears to any voices which suggest otherwise? If we dare suggest that significant segments of the leadership have fallen away from the truth, even as a theoretical possibility, our whole understanding of authority in the Church is called into question.

(b) What Saith the Church?

While such opinions are understandable they stand in opposition to both our history and to good theology. Our Church was founded in the first half of the sixteenth century during the time of the Reformation. The latter was a movement which was partly a protest against a church hierarchy that had lost its way and become corrupt in the extreme. A wide-spread call to return to a more biblical theology went unheeded by the authorized leadership of the church and the result was a tragic but inevitable (in the circumstances) open division in the church. As a result, the Reformers, English and otherwise, were forced to re-examine the nature of authority in the Church.

The English reformers, in their summary of the official doctrinal positions of Anglicanism known as the Thirty-Nine Articles (BCP pp. 698-714), joined with their contemporaries in reviving an ancient principle about authority. Article XXI, "Of the Authority of General Councils" holds that when such Councils are gathered together,

> ...(forasmuch as they be an assembly of men, whereof all be not governed with the Spirit and Word of God,) *they may err, and sometimes have erred in things pertaining unto God.* Wherefore things ordained by them as necessary to salvation have neither strength nor authority *unless it may be declared that they be taken out of holy Scripture*. (BCP, p. 706; my italics)

According to our history and to our theology as Anglicans the final test of what we are to believe and how we are to live is to hold the matter up to the Scriptures, not the pronouncements of individual leaders or those even of the whole Church. Our tradition speaks very clearly to this issue. As recently as the Lambeth Conference of 1968, the assembled bishops of our Communion once again affirmed that the Church is under Scripture and not the other way around.

Thus it is part of our Anglican heritage to maintain proper regard for our Church leaders within an overriding commitment to Scriptural truth. This last idea will be explored more fully below, but for the present purpose it is sufficient to stress that it is authentically Anglican to assume that even the great councils of the Church, traditionally regarded as the most authoritative of Church pronouncements, can error. From this perspective it is both wrong and dangerous to place Church leaders beyond criticism. This is the tradition out of which I wish to speak. I hope to do so in a spirit of love but I apologize in advance for those places where other attitudes are no doubt evident.

(c) What Saith the Scripture?

A deeper theological justification for proceeding as I have lies in the Scripture itself. Here one discovers the idea of a "faithful remnant" deeply rooted in the self-understanding of the Jewish people. Again and again in the history of Israel the official leadership of the nation, often a king, not only fell into occasional sin but was altogether evil. Just because they were in legitimate succession did not place them or their policies automatically in the will of God. In fact, it is clear that on many occasions they were leading the people into apostasy and idol worship. The prophets were sent to hold the leaders to account for straying from the revealed Word of God, especially as spelled out in the Law of Moses. In the meantime, it was acknowledged that not all of Israel had gone astray and there remained a smaller group within the nation known as the "remnant" which continued to serve God in spite of the official leadership. It was sometimes this stubborn perseverance which stayed the judgment of God upon the whole of the nation.

A similar situation is portrayed in the New Testament, especially in reference to our Lord's relationship with the official religious leadership of his day. It doesn't take much reading of the Gospels to perceive that Jesus himself regarded those in power as legitimate and deserving of respect but bereft of the Spirit. In fact, they often stood against the purposes of God. Ultimately they had Jesus put to death so vehement was their opposition. They thought that they were above the rabble who supported Jesus. After all, they were the rulers of the Temple and the doctors of the Law! (John 7:49) They had it so wrong that they thought Jesus must have been possessed by the chief of the demons. (Matt. 12:24)

This conflict continued through the life of the early church which eventually had to distinguish itself from Judaism in part because of such inflexibility. And even within the leadership of the early church Peter, the one chosen by our Lord himself, had to be opposed on the issue of circumcision for Gentile believers. It was only after Paul stood up to him at Antioch that Peter came around to the fuller truth (Gal. 2:11ff.).

The Bible therefore gives us ample warning against assuming that the official leadership of the Church is always in the right. Indeed, it almost seems at times that we should be *expecting* the leadership to go astray. As a result we should be on our guard both to support and encourage them when we can and also to confront them when necessary. This is not an easy thing to do because of the inherent complexities in the situation. However, it is a necessary thing, not only in our generation but in every generation.

(v) Conclusion: A Critical Path

There are, therefore, a number of good reasons to suggest that the path I have chosen is not to be avoided after all. There is much in our tradition that would encourage our taking it, even though it may be hard. While it may not be necessary in ordinary times, it is positively essential in times of crisis. For these reasons, then, I hope that I will be accorded the privilege both to speak and to be heard. I hardly expect everyone to agree with me! As well, I speak knowing that I, too, am a man under authority.

CHAPTER TWO

Crisis? What Crisis?

As he approached Jerusalem and saw the city, he wept over it and said, "If you, even you, had only known on this day what would bring you peace- but now it is hidden from your eyes." (Luke 19:41-2)

(i) Introduction: Reality Therapy

As I have already declared, a major reason for my speaking out at this time is my conviction that the Anglican Church of Canada is in a state of profound crisis. Unless action is taken there is a real danger that this once great institution, still rich with tradition and potential, will come to serious grief. This will result in significant loss not only to its members, but also to the entire Christian community in Canada. I will now explore the symptoms of this crisis as well as its effects upon the various segments of the Church. This will establish its reality in all our minds. This is the necessary first step toward recovery. In the course of this examination certain patterns will emerge, the most significant of which is the increasing fragmentization of the Church along a hundred different lines.

(ii) What Seems To Be the Problem?: Symptoms of the Crisis

(a) SYMPTOM 1: The Membership Blues

1) The Numbers Crunch

No church can exist without members. When membership is rising there is inevitably a sense of institutional well-being. When it is falling the opposite is true. Much of the sense of crisis in the ACC can be traced to this one hard truth: membership has been dropping steadily since the high point of the early1960's.

In 1961 there were 1,358,000 persons on the rolls and by 1994 this figure had been cut almost in half to 781,000. This precipitous drop in absolute numbers is bad enough but it took place while Canada's general population was growing. Thus, Anglicans went from being 7% of the population to only 3%. Admittedly these numbers are only a very rough guide to one's "place" in society but they have had a significant negative impact on the Anglican self-image. They also mask an even harder truth well known to anyone who is familiar with the maintaining of parish rolls: of the 781,000 officially listed as "members", a mere 171,000 were in church on an average Sunday in 1994! On this basis it is safe to conclude that active membership is really in the neighbourhood of only about 250,000, given the reasonable assumption that about two thirds of them would be present on any given Sunday.

2) The Other Shoe: Worse Yet To Come

While it is true that the rate of decline has slowed down recently, there is every reason to expect that this is merely the lull before the storm. This is the inescapable conclusion to any careful consideration of the particular composition of the current membership and how it came into being. *For a closer look soon reveals the startling truth that the contemporary Church is largely comprised of elderly females.* One has only to attend almost any Anglican service in any Anglican parish in order to verify this reality.

Since the 1960's there has indeed been a mass exodus but it is critical to understand that it has been mostly of younger people, while their elders have tended to remain faithful. This is born out by the statistics. While the membership as a whole declined by "only" 50% from 1961 to 1994, baptisms fell 60% and Sunday School attendance and confirmations fell a whopping 80%. Significantly, burials have only decreased by 15%. The Anglican population clearly has a hugely disproportionate number of older persons. It has not suffered a general decline in all categories. The lack of young people is an ominous sign for the future of the denomination. Unless things change considerably greater membership decline lies ahead. There is a real generation gap and the Church is in serious danger of falling into it in the near future.

It almost goes without saying that the graying membership of the Church is largely female. This is partly because females live longer than males and partly because in our society the Church has tended to attract more females than males. This is true of all denominations. However to Anglicans this means that there is going to be another painful fall in membership, the dropping of the other shoe as it were. When the younger generations left in the 1960's and 1970's there was a frightening drop in the numbers of Anglicans: the first shoe. Left behind in the Church were their parents, especially their mothers and grandmothers. The fact that they have lived so long has actually served to hide the true dimensions of the losses. But now the Anglican Church is facing a stark reality. These elderly females, faithful since the 1960's and who make up a great percentage of its membership, are going to pass away in the next ten to twenty years: the other shoe. Their natural replacements, their children and grandchildren, have vanished from the pew.

Knowledgeable predictions are that membership may shrink another fifty percent by the early years of the next century! Once all the "leftovers" from the boom years of the 1960's have died, the Church will finally bottom out at its natural sustainable level in contemporary society. The prospect of the membership being cut in half for the second time in fifty years is naturally sending tremors of angst throughout the denomination. It has enormous implications for every aspect of its life. Among other things it seems that significant cutbacks will have to take place both in the number of parishes and the clergy who serve them. This is not a pleasant prospect for the laity or for the clergy.

(b) SYMPTOM 2: Of Decayed Evangelism

1) The Avoidance Syndrome

Given the twin realities of serious past and future membership decline it would be natural to assume that the Anglican Church of Canada would be mobilizing all its energies toward the reversal of the situation. This does not appear to be what is happening. While it is true that some efforts have been made in the field of "membership development", they have met with only modest success. Oddly, some parishes have resisted even the mildest of suggestions that would make them more attractive and inviting to outsiders. Even installing such things as more readable signs out front or user-friendly coat rooms seems to be too much. Whatever one thinks of such efforts, even where employed they certainly do not seem to have made any significant impact on the numbers.

2) Other Possibilities

What is needed are *new* members. They are needed in large numbers if the Church is to avoid the kind of drastic and painful downsizing that is surely just around the corner (see Symptom 1). For Churches there are only a few possible sources of new members.

Traditionally it is the children of current members who step into the traces and take up the slack. As we have already seen, however, it is precisely the child-bearing age group that has already left or dropped out, taking their children with them. The advancing age of most Anglicans also precludes any serious expectation of a baby boom in the foreseeable future!

Another possibility it that the Church might acquire new members due to defections from other denominations. While it is true that the ACC has enjoyed modest "success" from this source, especially in reference to its clergy, there is nothing to suggest that it will bring significant numbers though the doors. The flow, as we have experienced it, is in exactly the opposite direction.

Next, we might remember that in the past Anglicans have benefited from the waves of new immigrants that have come to Canada. Much of New Brunswick, where I live, was originally settled by Loyalists escaping the American Revolution. Naturally they brought their Anglican faith with them. However, given the current patterns of immigration this is an unlikely possibility in our time. Perhaps things will change and there will be a mass influx of, say, Ugandans. To count on this for our salvation as a Church, however, would surely signal the depth of our desperation.

3) The Promise of Evangelism

There remains but one possible way of increasing Church membership: evangelism. By this I mean, at the most basic of levels, the changing of nominal Christians or of unbelievers into fully committed believers. Here, at least, there is serious potential! There are millions of unchurched Canadians and, according to Statistics Canada, even hundreds of thousands who still identify themselves as Anglicans but who are not active members of the Church. Not only is this true but it is generally acknowledged that there is a renewed interest in spiritual matters among Canadians. There seems to be an increasing dissatisfaction with the answers offered by science and technology to the deeper questions of life. So the pond is well stocked and the fish are biting.

Not only is the opportunity a very real one but the Christian church has had a history of success in the ministry of evangelism. The Early Church went from 120 to 3000 on one day and never looked back. Without a strong emphasis on the conversion of "pagans" to the faith, the history of Western civilization would have been considerably different. England itself would have remained a pagan nation and there never would have been a Church of England. While at times, as in the Crusades, this aspect of the mission of the Church was often misdirected, at times neglected, and usually entwined with cultural imperialism, it has nevertheless remained a vital characteristic of the faith. In the last century, with the expansion of the Empire there was a renewed emphasis on the evangelism of the newly encountered peoples of North America and elsewhere. The direct result of this effort is that the Anglican Church of Canada today has a very strong aboriginal component. To evangelize is a significant part of our history.

It is also part of our present, at least in other parts of the Anglican communion. In Kenya and in Chile, in Singapore and in Tegucigalpa, Anglicans are evangelizing with enthusiasm and with success, sometimes spectacular success. When the bishops of the communion last met at Lambeth in 1988 they affirmed evangelism as "the primary task" of the Church and committed the whole communion to a Decade of Evangelism in the 1990's.

4) The Reality of Evangelism

With all of this in mind it would seem logical to expect that the Anglican Church of Canada would have long ago mobilized a great effort directed at the evangelization of Canadian society. Sadly, this is not the case. There have been a few initiatives at the National level, mostly aimed at looking at ways to facilitate local evangelism. General Synod took a bit of its time to look at and discuss a video produced in association with the visit to Canada of the present Archbishop of Canterbury. It was entitled, prophetically for the ACC, "One Generation from Extinction". But within the overall agenda of General Synod, which dedicated hours and hours to the changing of Church structures, evangelism found itself at the back of the bus.

It is hard to escape the impression that, as a whole, the Church shows but a token interest in evangelism. Undoubtedly there is more talk than action. At least it was on the agenda of General Synod and did get discussed to some degree. But nothing was done to make it a priority. No great sums of money were dedicated to the task. It is difficult to see how the efforts of the National leadership will result in much evangelism actually being done.

5) Conclusion: No Way Out

So we are left with a Church that apparently has little or no prospect of reversing the membership loss that has already taken place or that will take place in the next few years. The usual means of increasing membership are either out of reach or, in the case of evangelism, virtually ignored. For some reason the Anglican Church of Canada, in a time of great pressure to find a way to add new members, it is unable or unwilling to evangelize. In so doing it is in effect sealing its fate. There appears to be no way of avoiding further drastic membership reduction and the trauma that will accompany it. This is surely an institution in serious crisis.

(c) SYMPTOM 3: The Falling Dollar

1) Treading Water

When parishioners by the thousands left the Anglican Church they naturally took their wallets with them! This would have had a crippling effect except for two additional developments. Those Anglicans who remained have done an exceptional job of reaching deeper into their pockets to support the Church. Although most parishioners are still a long way from tithing (giving the biblical 1/10 of their income) they are no longer merely token givers. This has enabled the Church not only to survive but to increase its spending considerably in spite of membership losses. There has also been an increasing dependence upon endowments left to the Church by the faithful departed: these, at least, have left their wallets behind! Without these gifts from the past many parishes would not be able to come close to balancing their budgets.

2) That Sinking Feeling

In spite of these developments, however, there is growing evidence that the denomination is settling into a serious financial crisis. Expenses have risen faster than inflation as clergy salaries and benefits, the major segment of parish budgets, have been raised to the level of other "professionals", maintenance of older buildings has become an ever-increasing burden, and Church bureaucracy, until very recently, has became something of a growth industry.

These factors, among others, combined with the continuing decline in membership (soon to speed up considerably), would suggest that current giving is very close to being "maxed out", if not in actually dropping. The modest response to recent appeals points in this same direction. Efforts are being doubled to convince an increasingly aging membership to leave its money to the Church in their wills. It does not stop there. The latest program involves persuading members to purchase life insurance which names the Church as both owner and beneficiary. The Communion of Saints will apparently require a very long offertory hymn! At the same time, because Anglicans do not yet approach the tithe in their giving (as Christians in some other denominations do), many Church officials remain convinced that the needed money "is still out there" in people's pockets. The problem is that few appear to be excited about giving it to the Church.

3) The Domino Effect

If this has created enormous stress at the parish level, the problem is even worse at the National and Diocesan levels. This is largely because of the way in which these levels of Church administration are funded. Individual Anglicans do not support these bureaucracies directly like citizens who send their taxes directly to the federal and provincial governments. Instead, they give only toward the budget of their own parish. The latter is then expected to forward part of its budgeted income to its own diocese as its "fair share" of diocesan expenses. The amount asked of each parish is determined by an agreed-upon formula.

In turn, the dioceses include the National Church as part of their budgets. Almost all of the National Church income comes from the dioceses. As a result of this system most parishioners are much more aware of the fact that the parish supports the diocese than they are of the fact that the diocese forwards a great proportion of that support to the National Church. For example, $407,144 out of the Diocese of Fredericton's total 1995 budget of $1,406,394 was to be sent to Toronto. In other words, well over one quarter of every dollar this diocese receives from its parishes is passed on to the National Church.

While such a system worked reasonably well in good times when parishes were able to pay their own expenses and still send significant "fair shares" to the diocese, it has proven very vulnerable when local expenses began to eat up more and more of parish budgets. The first thing to be cut is often the diocesan "fair share" because it is usually not seen as a necessary expense (as compared with the rector's stipend or the oil for the furnace). It is often a significant proportion of the parish budget and cutting it does not affect local program. Thus diocesan income takes a direct hit and it, in turn, finds its National apportionment an attractive item to cut for exactly the same reasons. In this way the National Church suffers disproportionately when financial times take a turn for the worse.

An editorial in the February 1996 *Anglican Journal* referred to this as the "domino effect". While indications are that parish income is at least holding its own if not increasing, diocesan income from the parishes is indeed falling. In turn dioceses are cutting the amounts they send on to the National level. The 1996 national apportionment budget was down almost $600,000 from the previous year. In spite of official denials to the contrary, there is little doubt that the recent "re-structuring" (down-sizing) of General Synod was at least in part forced on the institution because of this declining revenue. Bureaucracies, including church bureaucracies, have an innate drive to expand and contract only when compelled by outside forces. Given the likelihood of actual *cuts* in parish income (due to the anticipated attendance drop), we can expect the problem at the Diocesan and National levels to get a lot worse before it gets better, if it ever does. This has cast a very real pall over the Church's sense of well-being.

4) It's Every Parish for Itself

These trends are also part of the underlying and disturbing pattern of fragmentization that is taking place in the Anglican Church of Canada. There seems to be a definite rise in parochialism, as parishes become more focused on their own immediate needs and less on the needs of the wider Anglican community. The ties that bind the parishes to each other, to the diocese and to the National Church, seem to be much weaker than they have been in the past.

One often hears bishops referring to the diocese as the "basic unit of the church" but this is not a reality for most Anglicans. For them the basic unit is the parish. Perhaps we are evolving into congregationalists! While this may be too radical a conclusion, it does underline the sense in which our once-vaunted episcopal system of church government is under siege. Parishes are more interested in doing their own thing and this is part of what I mean by "fragmentization". The centre may not hold.

(d) SYMPTOM 4: Indecent Disorder

1) Introduction: The Trouble With Chaos

When a society or an institution is in trouble it invariably descends into chaos. While it may be going too far to claim that the Anglican Church of Canada is in chaos, there are enough indications of serious disorder to suggest that such a description will soon be all too appropriate. This disorder, which I have called fragmentization, is all more vivid when seen against the backdrop of Anglicanism's famous passion that "all things might be done decently and in order" (I Corinthians 14:40, KJV).

In what follows I will outline the main areas in which "indecent disorder" has taken hold. Each one is disturbing enough on its own but taken together the picture is truly alarming.

2) Uncommon Prayer

(A) The Way We Were

There is no question that liturgy is at the centre of Anglican life and identity. Up until quite recently it was the great pride of the Church that wherever you went in the worldwide Anglican Communion the worship in any parish church would be from the Book of Common Prayer. Canadians would return home from a trip to Australia and relate this phenomenon with warm amazement. Here they were on the other side of the world, able to worship with their accustomed familiarity. It made them feel at home and truly a part of a spiritual family that transcended geographic and political boundaries.

Most of this came about through the extension of the British Empire. Wherever it went the Prayer Book went as well. For a variety of reasons, including its deeply biblical theology and incomparable use of language, the Book of Common Prayer issued in 1662 became the established liturgy of the Church of England for three hundred years. While minor variations were introduced in different countries and over time, it remained largely intact. In Canada the last revision was in 1959.

(B) The Book of Alternative Services

With the arrival of the "liturgical renewal" movement of the early 1970's things began to change considerably. There was an assumption that after a period of experimentation the Church would authorize one set of contemporary services for common use. That is, the whole Canadian Church would settle down to worship either with the BCP or the new services or both. Most Anglicans could see the value in this even if they didn't agree with all the changes in "the new book". Most of these expectations seem to have been met with the publication of the Book of Alternative Services in 1985. True, the Church no longer was unified by liturgy but at least there was a sense that we could live with just the two patterns of common prayer. Those who desired worship in other contemporary forms, for example, were discouraged and told that they would have to convince the rest of the Church to revise the BAS before they could do so. Officially, at least, the Anglican instinct for common prayer was still alive.

Unofficially, however, it has been a different story. Even as the BAS was being introduced at least one diocesan bishop was telling his clergy that the ultimate goal of liturgical renewal was that each parish would have its own "do it yourself" liturgy! These would share a similar shape but would be largely customized to the needs and emphases of each particular congregation. He went on to demonstrate by leading the clergy in an "extempore" Eucharist, more or less making it up as he went. At the same time he followed the general pattern of eucharistic worship that had emerged from recent liturgical scholarship.

While this approach did not really catch on at the time, things have never the less continued to develop in the same direction. There are a number of evangelical parishes, for example, who were not happy with the BAS but still wanted a contemporary service. Some of them have just put together their own liturgy with or without the permission of their bishop. Others simply omitted or changed the portions of the BAS which caused offence. At the other end of the theological spectrum more radical liberals "experimented" with new liturgies that more directly reflected their concerns than did the BAS.

(C) Beyond the BAS

All of this has led to considerable pressure at official levels to push on beyond the BAS without actually revising the book itself . In fact, any revision has been deferred to the next century by the last General Synod. Judging by its other actions, however, we may be past the point of no return by then. The Evaluation Commission on the Book of Alternative Services recommended that supplementary material be prepared which would contain a number of different contemporary language eucharistic rites. One would be "inclusive in its language about God" (God as both "Father and Mother), one would "embody Reformed theological conscience" (the theology of the Book of Common Prayer in modern language) and one would "allow local communities to explore ways of including native spiritual traditions and other cultural expressions that are in keeping with Christian worship" (General Synod 1995 Report, p.10). General Synod accepted these recommendations and set in motion a process by which they can be implemented. Clearly the trend is going even further away from common prayer. It appears that each community within the Church is to have its own distinctive liturgy. This comes very close to the "do it yourself" liturgy envisioned above. There are so many things that liturgical revisers have begun both to say and to do that even the world itself could not contain the books that should be written.

While all of this may seem academic, to me as a parish priest it has ominous implications. For example, I am concerned about impact of all these changes on the pastoral care of older Anglicans. I, like many of our clergy, celebrate the Eucharist at a local nursing home. Nowadays this is such a common sight that it is almost unnoticed in the scheme of things. However, it is a focal point in the week for many of the residents. Church has been very important to them and they appreciate still being part of its life. What is less obvious, perhaps, is the role of the Book of Common Prayer. Although they come from various parishes, all the Anglican residents are intimately familiar with it. Not being able to see or hear so well presents no real barrier. They know the liturgy by heart. Few of us who conduct these services can remain unmoved by the way in which this enables even enfeebled minds to participate. It is an experience soon to vanish, both for the residents and for the officiant. In future years Anglicans will be arriving at the nursing home having used a variety of liturgies within their own parish. Not only so, but this variety will have been a different mix from parish to parish. When the residents assemble for worship yearning for the security of the familiar, what will they encounter?

For three hundred years the Book of Common Prayer served as the glue that held the entire Anglican Communion together. Now, a mere decade after its introduction, the Book of Alternative Services is seen as obsolete by many that hailed its arrival. It is clear that, once loosed, the dogs of liturgical revision cannot be controlled. They have savaged the very idea of common prayer and, with it, much of the sense of unity and identity it gave to the Church. Those days are gone, perhaps forever. Instead liturgy is fast developing into "uncommon prayer" and is well on the way to becoming the outward and visible sign of inward and spiritual division. One thing is certain: we must look beyond liturgy for any signs of unity.

(3) Hymns and Hers

(A) The Days of "Common Praise"

One of the former signs of Anglican unity and order was the fact that the vast majority of the parishes not only worshipped with one liturgy but they also sang from one book. From the largest cathedrals to the lowliest of country churches one found neatly arranged pairs of "red books" (BCPs) and "blue books" waiting the arrival of worshippers. Nowadays the average pew rack is much more cluttered. You might find, in addition to the "red book" and the "blue book", a "green book", a larger "red book" (making the little "red book" into the "wine book"), a colourful spiral bound book and even some photocopied material. And then, if you weren't careful, your wandering eye might notice the overhead projector with its pile of transparencies! You could be forgiven a nostalgic smile if you were to read the full title of the "blue book": "The Book of Common Praise, Being *the* Hymn Book of the Anglican Church of Canada"!

Just as common prayer is fast becoming a thing of the past so also is common praise. It is probably true to say that for the vast majority of parishes the "blue book", last revised in 1938, was the only hymn book until the early 1970's. It was then "replaced" by "The Hymn Book of the Anglican Church of Canada and the United Church of Canada", the infamous "red book". This joint effort, arising in a time when church union was under discussion, found a welcome home in many parishes but certainly not in all. Some bought it only to regret their decision later when they realized that many of the old favourites were left out or had unfamiliar tunes and the newer hymns proved unattractive. Others simply ignored it altogether. One thing is for sure: it never became *the* hymn book. It was misnamed from the beginning and it seemed to fade away with the failure of the attempt to bring the two churches together. After this the official hymnody of the Church went into a long period in which there was little change.

(B) A Different Drummer

Unofficially, however, much was happening indeed. Much of the Church, mainly from the traditional/orthodox side, came under the broad influence of the "renewal" movement. Trans-denominational in scope, this phenomenon has produced a wide variety of music in response to its emphasis on more expressive worship. We find choruses, songs and hymns written in a bewildering variety by a large number of talented authors and musicians, from Graham Kendrick to Timothy Dudley-Smith to Michael Baughan. Much of this music has become very popular at the grassroots level and requires something other than organ to support it. Worship teams have been developed to lead the congregation with piano, keyboard, guitar, trumpet and even drums. While not too many Anglican parishes have gone this full route, many have taken up this music with enthusiasm. Much of it is written in contemporary music styles and is thus more directly plugged into modern life than the older hymns.

Because renewal music is so broadly based and is in constant development, it cannot be contained in any one "hymn" book. By the nature of the music, any such publication is soon out of date. In this climate it is every parish for itself. It has to pick and choose its way through the various offerings. At one extreme many have found the British compilation "Mission Praise" to be helpful, containing as it does a good selection of older hymns along with some of the more tested modern efforts. At the other end of the spectrum some parishes buy a copyright license and mix and match from a number of different sources for any particular service. It is quite possible for an Anglican who is reasonably familiar with this kind of music to visit a parish and encounter music which she has never heard before. Fortunately it is usually catchy and easy to learn.

(C) Hymns Without Hims

Meanwhile, back at the official level changes were also afoot. In 1986 the National Executive Council set up a Hymn Book Task Force. This group reported back to the 1995 General Synod with a proposed collection of hymns and was authorized to complete the preparation of the book for presentation to the Council of General Synod for permission to publish.

While there are a number of reasons for this initiative, the one that shall concern us here is the desire to provide the Church with hymns that conform to modern sensibilities about the use of inclusive language. The editors have, however, moved much beyond the commonly accepted practice of using inclusive language in reference to human beings. They have altered the language about God her/him/itself! This has required significant modification of many familiar hymns. In the hymn "Joyful, joyful we adore thee", for example, the line that reads "Thou our Father, Christ our Brother" becomes "Thou(!) our Father and our Mother". Enormous effort has gone into the attempt to avoid the "masculinity" of both God the Father and God the Son. Naturally with such an approach there is a subsequent vagueness when it comes to the Trinity. The more radical changes occur in some of the new hymns that have been selected. One proclaims that God is "Womb of life and source of being" while another refers to "her" as "Sophia". The latter is the Greek word for "Wisdom" which the Bible sometimes personifies as female. The major justification for using it as a term for God comes from the Apocryphal book entitled the Wisdom of Solomon, not the Bible. To use the untranslated "Sophia" may be questionable also in that many feminists are promoting the worship of the Greek goddess of the same name.

The convener of the Task Force has indicated that "...the (new) hymn book is a collection of diverse voices, which speak in different ways to different people." As if to underline this reality, some of the hymns are apparently to be published with alternative words for the more (or less) adventurous! It seems that, in this forum, at least, some of our division will be on display for everyone to see. This idea of "diversity" is a limited one, however. excluding as it does those who take offense at the presence of some of these new elements. Many Anglicans will be uninterested in buying and using a hymn book that would force them to say less than they want to say about God or to use language that is not their own. Another glaring exclusion from the book is renewal music. Thus at least two significant "voices" in the Church are silenced. The bottom line is that only a portion of the Church will be served by this new hymn book and it certainly does not even attempt to restore a sense of unity through worship. "Diversity", narrowly defined, is the word. It may be just another word for division.

At best this new hymn book will be jammed into the pew rack along with all its mothers, fathers, sisters and brothers. Perhaps another colour would be helpful! There is just too much going on in the modern world of worship music to expect anything approaching standardization. The old ideal of "common praise" is further away than ever. It rests in pieces.

4) Curriculum, Curricula

(A) Sunday School Daze

Any large organization wanting to ensure that its new members would grasp its purpose and methods would provide them with a vigorous and uniform program of instruction. In this way they could be shaped and molded to take their place in the overall efficient operation of the enterprise. Without such training the membership would soon have little sense of a common cause or shared goals. Eventually such an organization would find itself falling into chaos and unable, as a result, to function properly.

Recognizing this truth has led many Christian denominations to produce a standard Sunday School curriculum for use in all their congregations. Each member then has a common educative experience which helps create a shared understanding of the Faith and leads to a profound sense of unity, even among a widely scattered flock.

Such was the historical experience of the Anglican Church of Canada. Through its General Board of Religious Education (G.B.R.E.) an extensive Sunday School curriculum was made available to the parishes of the denomination. By all accounts it was almost universally used and made a significant contribution to the sense of being part of the same Church. In some areas teachers from various parishes would even get together on a regular basis in order to prepare themselves for upcoming lessons and work out any problems. Reading it today one is struck, almost amazed, by both its breadth and depth. It is hard to imagine a modern Church providing such a rigorous and thoroughgoing education for its younger members. The teachers manual for each grade came in a lengthy hardback volume. It is clear that a great deal was expected of both teacher and student. Any child passing through such a system would be well on her way to a good start in the Christian life.

The difference in the scene today could not be more profound. There is no longer any denominational Sunday School curriculum. Instead there are only curricula, plural, and they have to be obtained from sources outside the Anglican Church. A significant number of parishes are using the "Whole People of God" curriculum which originates in the United Church. Others may be using the "Teale" curriculum independently developed in the Episcopal Church, the increasingly popular "Bible Way" from the Christian Reformed Church or one of a wide variety of interdenominational evangelical curricula. It is literally every Sunday School superintendent for himself. Needless to say any sense of unity derived from the use of a common curriculum has long since vanished.

The change seems to have started with the introduction of the so-called "New Curriculum" in the early sixties. This was apparently meant to replace the G.B.R.E. program of previous generations now thought to be dated and in need of complete revision. Unfortunately, the new program was not terribly well received and within a decade it had vanished along with the G.B.R.E. itself. That part of the National Church which is responsible for Christian education has been reduced to a shadow of its former self, almost completely absorbed by a larger committee. Into the vacuum have swept these various contenders for the crown but so far there is no clear winner. Instead, the fragmentization of the denomination as a whole continues through its

Sunday Schools, leaving less and less likelihood that they will be able to make any contribution to a common vision.

(B) Font of Knowledge?

When we turn to other educational programs beyond the Sunday School the picture becomes even more confused. Here, in the absence of any solid statistical information, one is forced to rely on personal experience and observation. It is important to keep the attendant weaknesses of such an approach firmly in mind.

It is true to say that there has been a welcome movement in the denomination towards providing an educational process for those seeking baptism for themselves or their children. This comes out of a renewed understanding of the importance of baptism as the fundamental moment of entry into the Church. The problem is that this "educational process" seems to be different in every parish! Few dioceses, if any, have a common approach, although it is likely that if proper studies were done certain common patterns would emerge. It is clear, however, that such programs range from the rigorous to the undemanding. One of the tensions between clergy is created by the fact that in one parish those seeking baptism might have to attend a course for a number of months and wait until a given Sunday for the service while in the parish next door the rector is willing to baptize more or less "on request" with little or no preparation.

Regardless of the method or form of instruction there remains the question of its content. Here we have an even bigger question mark. The truth is that no one knows what baptismal candidates in the Anglican Church of Canada are being taught about the faith. This is usually, if not always, left up to the individual rector and reflects his or her understanding and emphasis. Given the wide divergences here, it is safe to assume that this diversity is reflected in the entry level educational process, whatever its form.

(C) Confirmation Confusion

Confirmation preparation presents a similar scenario. In days gone by it was understood that one had to memorize the Catechism in order to be confirmed. On page 544 of the Book of Common Prayer we are told in capital letters that this Instruction is "to be learned by every person before he be brought to be confirmed by the Bishop". This is now largely ignored. Certainly it would shock most candidates to be asked by a bishop even to recite the Apostle's Creed. What is being done instead? Who knows? Most rectors make a conscientious effort to prepare their candidates as best they can but there is little commonality observable. They are on their own.

To make matters even more complicated and to once again show how divided the denomination really is, it is necessary to observe that there is a vigorous internal debate going on about the very nature and place of Confirmation in the modern church. It used to be that one had to be confirmed in order to receive Holy Communion. However, the renewed emphasis on baptism as the full initiation rite has led to the communication not only of unconfirmed children but even of infants in some parishes. This has obviously removed the major reason for Confirmation. Many continue to see it as a valid opportunity for a person to take on his or her baptismal vows in a personal way but have opened the question about the proper age at which it should be undertaken. Oddly, this has resulted in one side saying it really is for children when they reach the age of "accountability" (perhaps as young as six or seven but always variable with each child), while the other would have it delayed until one's basic vocation in life has been chosen (perhaps as old as twenty-five or so depending again on the individual circumstances). So we have some advocates of around age seven, others around age twenty-five and still others wishing to retain the traditional age of around thirteen! At least one diocese has, in response to all this, announced its intention to "suspend" confirmations altogether! To say the contemporary Church does not enjoy a common mind on this once-settled topic is to engage in serious understatement. Again, our fragmentization is evident.

(D) The Twilight Zone

When one turns to the issue of Anglican adult Christian education things get murkier yet. The unfortunate pattern has been to treat Confirmation as kind of a graduation exercise after which there was no particular expectation or provision for continuing education. It is almost unheard of, for example, for an Anglican parish to have an adult Sunday School class. It may surprise many Anglicans to discover that this is routine in other denominations. Many parishes try to fill the gap by promoting the practice of daily devotions through the use of material provided by Scripture Union or Forward Movement. Others have a Bible Study group, usually led by the rector for a faithful few. In addition, groups come together on an occasional basis (often in Lent) to study particular issues. Some bring in a lecturer or a missioner from time to time as well. The best that many can offer is a book or pamphlet rack at the back of the church. But as far as a systematic approach to adult continuing Christian education is concerned, it is largely non-existent. Again, where it does exist, there is not only a variety of forms, there is a variety of content. The picture is truly bewildering.

5) Conclusion: Not All It's Cracked Up to Be

Bewildering. That would be the word. Unless one wanted to use "confusing", "chaotic", "inconsistent", "fragmented", "complicated" or at best, "variegated", "diverse" or even "flexible". Whichever word one chooses, none can bear the weight of unity. To the extent that one might hope for a sense of unity to come through or be encouraged by the life of the local Church one is clearly in for a serious disappointment. If anything the opposite is true.

Our educational scene, for example, is a clear reflection of the division that is characteristic of the whole denomination. Even worse, in turning our backs on the denominational Sunday School curriculum, we have abandoned the one common denominator that we did have in this area. So also we have no common liturgy or praise. Any of these, like so much of our past, seems beyond imagining, let alone beyond recovering.

It is difficult to remember that not that long ago a newspaper editor could have sent his reporters into all the Anglican parishes in his city on a particular Sunday and each one would come back with the same story. The congregations were worshipping with the same liturgy, singing from the same hymn book, listening to the same anthems, reading the same portions of Scripture and having their children taught from the same lessons.

Picture, if you can, the common bond this shared experience could create between complete strangers coming together for wider Church meetings. While there would certainly be differences of opinion they would nevertheless share a common outlook and this would enable them to work together.

Today, reporters returning from a similar assignment would be a very confused lot when they compared notes. They would have experienced the modern Anglican reality: the "smells and bells" of a Prayer Book anglo-catholic celebration of high mass, the sweetgrass smoke of a native circle, the raised hands of boisterous charismatics praising Jesus on the overhead and using the BAS, the relaxed informality of an evangelical congregation with a do-it yourself liturgy and even a gathering of "womin" (as they call themselves) whose experimental liturgy seems to be more focussed on Sophia than on Jesus. Each of these services employ different hymn-books and use different musical accompaniment from pipe organ to small band to guitar to native drums.

What would complete strangers coming from such radically diverse parish environments might have in common? Ask them to work together on a wider church basis and see what happens. What happens is the current crisis in the Church. It is no mystery.

Now it can be argued that the diversity within the Anglican Church of Canada is no more than that which the church has always experienced. After all, the Christians gathered for the great council at Nicea in 325 A.D. looked and sounded a lot different from those gathered at the great missionary congress at Exeter Hall, London in 1840. This is true. The Gospel has adapted itself to hundreds, perhaps thousands, of different cultures. But it is also true that no one tried to put all these different expressions of Christianity into the same organizational body and expect them to function well together! Difficult as such a challenge would have been in the past, it pales beside the one facing the ACC.

If it were only a matter of "different expressions" of the one faith, as at Nicea and at London, there might be some hope of eventually discovering common ground in the essential truths of that faith. In other words one could theoretically distinguish between form and content, between outward appearance and inward reality. However, as the next chapter will demonstrate, much of the diversity in the Anglican Church can be traced to the fact that the "common ground in the essentials of the faith" is simply no longer present in the institution. This threatens to make any effort to discover an underlying unity an exercise in futility.

(f) SYMPTOM 5: A Complex Superiority

1) A Vested Interest

In a healthy organization the leadership is ever attentive to the needs and desires of its membership. This is a basic rule. Violate it and you are in big trouble. Because of it is we find politicians poring over the latest poll results with great care and paying vast sums to those who can devise and interpret them. Another critical leadership function is to be able to communicate vision and direction for the organization in such a way that it gathers the enthusiastic support of the membership. The latter must feel an important part of the whole enterprise by being consulted, informed and empowered.

From this perspective there are many signs that the Anglican Church of Canada is indeed in big trouble. A large gap has opened up between the person in the pew and the clergy elite who provide the leadership. The Christian church, in almost all of its manifestations, has struggled with "clericalism", the dominance of the clergy. This is nothing new. But in the Anglican Church it appears to be especially virulent, making a very real contribution to the present crisis. Speaking as an insider on this issue I can testify that, at our worst moments, many clergy seem convinced that only what we do and what we are concerned about have true significance in the life of the Church. Indeed, this is what we often mean when we talk about what "is going on in the Church". The rank and file membership often appear merely as a backdrop to the real drama. This, I would reiterate, is at our worst moments! But they are real ones, human ones, that often result in our seeing things from a very narrow career-oriented perspective.

As a newly ordained clergy person I was soon initiated into this way of thinking by listening to a conversation among a number of more senior clergy about a colleague who had once again found himself unable to function in a parish due to his own incompetence. The discussion centred solely around the need to find him another parish so that he could continue to have an income and a career. Almost no sympathy was expressed for the poor parishioners either of his last parish or the future one where he would undoubtedly wreak the same havoc again. The thought of turfing him out on his ear was simply considered unchristian. There is some truth to this, of course. But surely it is even more unchristian to entrust the cure of souls to an incompetent priest. It is very easy to fall into this mindset as a clergy person because it is obviously in your own self-interest to do so: once you are in the club you have a high degree of job security. I am ashamed to say that I am as guilty as anyone of finding comfort in this view. It is the perspective of the elite.

2) Staying Power

Elitism is about power. Who has it and who keeps it. The clergy-elite in the Anglican Church is exceptionally powerful. The numbers tell the story. Back in 1961, when the Church was at its greatest numerical strength of 1,320,000 it was served by 1,711 parish clergy. By 1994 membership had dropped almost in half to 780,000, but the number of clergy had only dropped to 1,622. While it would be unfair to attribute this remarkable fact solely to the power of the clergy-elite it does suggest that they have been able to maintain their numbers in the face of obvious economic pressure. When one considers that the average stipend and benefits package has increased dramatically over the same period the accomplishment is all the more impressive.

3) A Little Knowledge is a Dangerous Thing

But it is not just about numbers. It is about influence and direction. The clergy, as the authorized leadership in the church, have always enjoyed (and deserved) a certain amount of respect and even veneration. The title of "Reverend" is a natural reflection of this truth. In those branches of the church, like Anglicanism, that retain a more Catholic order this tendency towards veneration seems to be more marked than in those following a congregational model. The high regard for the clergy in all Christian Churches is fundamentally a reflection of both the biblical pattern and the natural human need for hierarchical leadership. It is not wrong but it does have its dangers.

In Anglicanism this tendency to put the clergy on a pedestal was heightened by the Catholic revival of the last century. At that time the term "Father", as a proper title for the priest, was brought back into the Church from pre-Reformation days. At its best this title highlights both the responsibilities of anyone entrusted to the care of Christ's flock and the honour due to this office.

Unfortunately, the use of "Father" can also serve a much less worthy agenda, one that keeps the "children" in ignorance and dependence. This is all too common a feature of Anglican Church life even among those who avoid the use of Father as a title. It is marked by an almost complete lack of serious interest in the religious education of the laity. Sermons have become "homilies" and clergy even boast about how short they can make them. From one perspective, at least, this is a indication that lay people are best seen only in a secondary or supporting role. There is no real need for them to be educated or knowledgeable in matters of the faith.

We need to realize, however, that knowledge is power. The ignorant are subject to manipulation by the knowledgeable. It is a dangerous situation for both sides: one is tempted to control and the other to resent being controlled. While there is no evidence that the maintenance of a relatively ignorant laity has resulted from any conscious effort, it is a reality nevertheless. A sad reality.

4) Left is Right

There is also an obvious cleavage between the leadership of the Anglican Church of Canada and its membership in the arena of public life, of politics, economics and social policy. There was a time when the ACC could have been said to be the Conservative Party at prayer. While that is still generally true of the rank and file, the clergy-elite has taken a radical veer to the left, taking positions on issue after issue that are virtually indistinguishable from those of the New Democratic Party. This has contributed substantially to the alienation that many members have towards their Church. They have been astounded as leaders of a religious body who have little experience of the business world have poured invective on capitalism while being decidedly friendly towards the totalitarian regimes of world communism. Many proclamations of solidarity with leftist revolutionaries were issued while few, if any, were supportive of the millions of victims of Mao or Stalin. While the amateur dictator of Chile (a rightist) was seen as the devil incarnate, the consummate professional, Fidel Castro (a communist), was seen as benevolent. Indeed, the latter is still defended, especially in opposition to the United States which often appears as the enemy of all that is good and right.

Furthermore Church leaders consistently identified leftist analysis and solutions as self-evidently more Christian than any other. One could not be in true solidarity with the poor unless one adopted a socialist solution to their plight. Meanwhile the people in the pew were forced to deal with their own reality and found themselves pushed further and further away from their leaders. In fact sociologist Reginald Bibby, in his 1986 study of the Diocese of Toronto entitled "Anglitrends", reported (p. 11) that ordinary Anglicans were only half as likely to support the socialist NDP than were the rest of the population! Eighty-one percent voted Conservative (56%) or Liberal (25%). The gap between leaders and members in this area has no doubt widened even further with the collapse of the Soviet empire (making its corruption and oppression a matter of public record) and the general disarray of democratic socialism in the West (leaving its relevance to mainstream society an open question at best).

5) Starting From the Top

One undoubted characteristic of elitism is that initiatives for change originate at the top of the organization rather than at the bottom. It is difficult to imagine an institution that better fits this pattern than the Anglican Church of Canada. With few exceptions one is hard-pressed to name any recent change that has developed at the insistence of those at the grassroots. In fact, in most instances, the changes have met with at least bewilderment if not outright resistance from this level.

The classic example of this is the process which led to the introduction of the Book of Alternative Services. There was no discernible push for modern liturgies from the person in the pew. No petitions were circulated among parishioners calling for revisions to the Book of Common Prayer. Whatever the merits of the proposed new liturgy, from beginning to end its introduction was an initiative "from above". Certainly a concerted effort was made to obtain input and feedback from as wide a range of Anglicans as possible but many who participated in the process felt that they were nevertheless ignored. The evangelical community, for example, submitted weighty critiques of the proposed Eucharistic Prayers but to no avail. The leadership of the Church was fully aware that these Anglicans has serious objections and yet the Book was published anyway.

This is the behaviour of an elite. It assumes that it has the proper perspective from which the good of all can be pursued. Surrounded by the like-minded and having discounted other possibilities as outmoded or even dangerous, such groups show a marked tendency to filter out those things that do not fit into their agenda. This behaviour is largely unconscious and is almost certainly unintended. This, however, does not make the pain it inflicts any less real, as anyone who reads the "Letters to the Editor" section of the Anglican Journal can testify.

But even worse was to come when the BAS was finally issued and introduced into parishes. The official line, which was followed by many, held that the BAS was only an alternative to the BCP. Nevertheless in diocese after diocese there was pressure from above, often not at all subtle, to introduce and use this book in spite of the wishes of the rector or the people. In many other parishes, rectors eager for change assigned the BCP to the early Communion while the main service was exclusively BAS (and exclusively Holy Communion, but that is another story- cf. "What Happened to Morning Prayer?" by Alan Hayes and John Webster and available from the Prayer Book Society). In at least one diocese the bishop had to point out to his clergy that this was *not* an acceptable interpretation of "alternative"! Diocesan services often became exclusively BAS. These impositions caused much unrest and even heartache as the beloved BCP began to disappear from use. Many, perhaps even thousands, have left the church or have become inactive because of this one issue. Within a year of the BAS's debut, Reginald Bibby reported in *Anglitrends* that 31% of less active Anglicans cited changes in styles of worship as a key factor in their alienation (p. 94). This is not to imply that the BAS was always and everywhere introduced with insensitivity or rejected with vehemence. However there does appear to have been a widespread pattern of the clergy-elite going in one direction and the people going along reluctantly at best.

6) Conclusion: Elusions of Grandeur

There are many complexities in this. Perhaps, as a Church, we need to ask ourselves afresh, "What is the kind of relationship between the clergy and the laity that will best enable each to realize their full potential in Christ?" Many gifts have been given but we don't seem to know how to recognize or use them without feeling threatened on the one hand or fearful of failure on the other. To return to the useful image of the "Father", the better ones know their task remains unfulfilled until their children grow to maturity and take their place in the world. There is much evidence that such an understanding of Fatherhood has eluded too many, both ordained and lay, in the Anglican Church of Canada.

(iii) A Plague On All Our Houses: The Effects of the Crisis

How are the three "houses" of the Anglican Church of Canada, bishops, clergy and laity, experiencing the crisis that has been outlined? What we find will be yet further evidence that the crisis exists and that it is serious indeed.

(a) The Mood in the House of Bishops :The Silence of the Shepherds

1) Introduction: Quiet in the House

It might seem odd, on the face of it, to have to try to provide evidence that such a crisis really does exist. After all, it should be perfectly obvious to any observer if things are as serious as I allege. One would normally expect such a crisis to be front and centre at the Church's official gatherings, especially at the House of Bishops and the General Synod. Part of the responsibility of leadership is precisely crisis management. But there is only silence. If my analysis is reasonably accurate, this silence would mean that the highest level of leadership of the Church (mainly focused on the Bishops in our system) is either unaware of the crisis or is in some form of denial about it. What follows will explore the evidence as to which of these is true. It is my conviction that it is more a state of denial than anything else. I will conclude with an effort to explain how this could be, given the overwhelming evidence that the Church is indeed in crisis.

2) All Together Now

To begin with it is necessary to explore one of the legitimate reasons, perhaps, for the silence. There is a deep commitment to "collegiality", especially at the level of the House of Bishops. This means that unless they can speak with one voice they prefer not to speak at all. There are some good reasons for this approach but from the perspective of this chapter three problems present themselves.

There are some issues over which the bishops remain divided while at the same time it is clear that momentum inside and outside the House is building to go in one direction or the other. The silence of those bishops and other leaders who are opposed to the trend amounts to consent. They will soon be overtaken by events outside their control. Secondly, it is possible to wonder out loud whether or not such "collegiality" amounts to an abdication of leadership. Where are the leaders who will stand up and say "Thus sayeth the Lord!"? Although our leadership often affirms the unchanging nature of the doctrine of the Church, it rarely, if ever, articulates that doctrine. One is left assuming that the teaching of the Church is just not relevant to modern Christians or that the leadership cannot, in fact, agree on that teaching. Thirdly, "collegiality" often gives a false impression of unity. What place does such a practice have in an institution which is supposed to uphold Christian values of openness and honesty? To persist in it may even contribute to a climate of suppression as dissenters to the majority opinion are forced into silence.

3) Are We In Denial?

(A) What the Primate Said

To return to the main line of argument, the first piece of evidence that suggests that the leadership of the Church is in denial about the current crisis arises out of some recent remarks of the Primate (Anglican Journal, February 1997). He was responding to the fact that almost an entire parish on Vancouver Island decided to disassociate itself from the Anglican Church. To many Anglicans this is an extremely momentous event and should have set alarm bells off all across the Church. What is going on here? While this situation will be dealt with in greater detail in Chapter Six (see "Reaching a Critical Mass", p. 133), at the present time it is of critical importance to note that, according to the highest official in the Church, it has no more implication than "...one parish is unhappy with the actions of General Synod" and represents only "...a small group of people from one part of the country." Assuming that this is not merely the statement of a politician trying to keep the lid on a dangerous situation, it seems that the Primate is unaware of how many Anglicans are in sympathy with the same frustrations that led to this unfortunate development.

The reality is that there are many thousands in this category all across the country. In fact there are several whole dioceses which have taken actions which strongly indicate that they share a similar point of view. It is unfortunate that the Primate was unable, because of the visit to Canada of the Archbishop of Canterbury, to be present at Essentials 94 when 700 Anglicans who were generally of this opinion gathered in an effort to call the Church back to its biblical roots. If he could have been there to observe and to talk and to listen he would have a better understanding of both the breadth and depth of the alienation many are experiencing in the Church. But is the Primate truly unaware of all this? If he is, the elitism of the leadership, its isolation from the grassroots, has reached extremely dangerous proportions. If he is not, then he may be, like most of us, in a state of denial over the true condition of the Church.

(B) What the Delegate Said

The second piece of evidence arises out of a recently published report from one of the delegates to the last General Synod. The author has been involved at the highest levels of administration in her own diocese and is as knowledgeable as anyone about what is really going on in the Church. She was struck by the faith and commitment of the members of Synod and that one could "...easily come away with a glowing feeling that as Anglicans we have it all right...". But that was not the reality as she soon discovered:

> Each day during meal times and afterhour gatherings, I met and spoke with Anglicans from big cities, farming communities, northern company towns, native reserves, and small town Canada. When we got past the initial chatty exchanges, inevitably the story was the same. Smaller congregations, shrinking budgets, the absence of young people, burn out - not only of the clergy but overworked lay volunteers, loss of spirit, and, in general, all the signs of a real crisis. General Synod was not about to address any of those issues. Instead, the Synod spent nine hours hearing presentations, meeting in caucus, and debating a new Strategic Plan' for the structure and function of the National Church. This plan, called 'Preparing the Way', ...was about management, not leadership, which the Church seems to be looking for but can't find. (INCOURAGE, October 1995, p. 2)

What is striking about this account is the contrast between the kinds of concerns on the minds of the ordinary members of General Synod and those of its leadership. It is almost as if they were living in two different worlds. However, it is clear that the "lambs" are not silent even if the shepherds are! Most involved Anglicans know very well that their Church is in a serious crisis even if we are not prepared to say it out loud and in public. It is not only the subject of the table-talk at General Synod but wherever two or three Anglicans are gathered together for conversation, there it is in the midst of them! It is the reality in which we live and move and have our being.

In such circumstances one would expect the Church to be mobilizing itself to deal with the crisis in all its dimensions. Our money and intellectual resources would be poured into the search for solutions. Instead there is silence. The evidence strongly suggests that the lack of official response to the crisis cannot be on account of ignorance on the part of leadership. That we are in crisis is indeed "common" knowledge. Why then the silence? Could it be that there is a realization, conscious or unconscious, that the enormity of our fundamental and irreconcilable division is just too difficult to face?

(C) What the Strategic Plan Said

That the answer to this last question might be "yes" is suggested by a third piece of evidence that indicates that the Church's leadership is aware not only of the crisis but also of its inability to do much about it. This is to be found in the nature of the "Strategic Plan" entitled "Preparing the Way" (see *General Synod 1995 Report*). In essence this is an attempt to reorganize the administration of the Church by downsizing at the National level in the expectation that those tasks no longer undertaken will be picked up at lower levels in the structure. In the words of the official Report of the proceedings of General Synod this is all part of a plan to "...focus vision in the location that will make the best use of resources." (p. 3) The National Church will thus be allowed "...to do what it does well, mission, partnership, and self-sufficiency, and allowing the dioceses to do the rest." (p. 3)

There is great significance in this move. It is not just a matter of being forced to trim the budget because of obvious financial difficulties. In fact those responsible for developing this "vision" specifically denied that it was shaped by budgetary considerations. While this denial is taken with a grain of salt by many, there is good reason to pay careful attention to the implications of what has been done.

In the secular world this kind of restructuring is known as "downloading". We see it often as the federal government tries to trim its budget by doing fewer tasks things, forcing the provincial governments to take up the slack. In turn the provinces do the same to municipalities. While again this appears to be budget-driven, in fact what is happening is a massive shift away from the commitment to a strong central government in favour of more local responsibility. This same de-centralization is now taking place in the Church. While there are good and bad aspects to this, for our purposes it is sufficient to note that this fits very nicely into the overall pattern of fragmentization. It is, in fact, a formal recognition that this fragmentization has taken place and that we have less and less in common as an institution. Just as our nation is fragmenting into ever smaller "communities", so also is the Church. These new structures merely reflect this new reality.

But there is more to it than that. There is in these structural changes a tacit admission that the National Church has been simply unable to solve the myriad problems facing the denomination and is quietly passing many of them on down to lower levels of administration in the hope that they can be better addressed there. Our above-quoted delegate put it like this:

> Our prayer must be that with a new structure, the national operation of the General Synod has now been updated and streamlined and will function more efficiently with fewer staff, smaller committees, and ultimately, less money. *The rest of our problems must be dealt with in our dioceses and parishes with our finest and best resource - each and every one of the faithful in the pew. This is where our leadership will come from and we need to recognize that.* (INCOURAGE, October 1995, p. 2- my italics)

This quotation captures precisely the nature of the changes that have come upon us as well as the implication that our current leadership has passed on to others the responsibility for solving our current crisis. It is certainly possible to interpret these events as a tacit admission of failure. Unable to provide the Church with any real solution to its problems, those at the top have "discovered" the neglected reservoir of local wisdom.

Of course this begs a number of questions, including especially the preparedness of those in the pew to deal with the perplexing and long-ingrained problems facing the Church. Like the provincial and municipal governments, the local levels of the Church may be overwhelmed by their new responsibilities. One suspects that this shift may only turn out to be an exercise in wishful thinking. With no particular plan in mind, Church officials are hoping against hope that local solutions will arise from the ashes of now distant dreams. The likelihood of this happening is not certain. What is clear is that leadership will not be coming from above.

4) Conclusion: No Denying It

If, then, we are facing a crisis of unnerving proportions, this attempt to pass the buck (but not the bucks!) to the local level could be seen as an abdication of responsibility. However, this is surely much too harsh a judgment. The options that face us are so stark that there is no disgrace in avoiding them. *The truth is that no one knows what to do!* In fact, it is part of my thesis that nothing *can* be done until the fundamental division that underlies the whole Church is squarely faced. Naturally no one wants to do this. It is just too terrible a truth.

There no doubt comes a stage in the life of a declining institution where things seem so bad that attention cannot be drawn to them without calling the future of the whole institution into question. The silence of the shepherds does not necessarily mean, therefore, that I am mistaken in my estimation of the crisis we face. Rather this strange silence, *given the reality of the situation*, forms a major piece of the evidence that I am not far wrong. It will take enormous courage simply to emerge from denial.

(b) The Mood in the House of Clergy: The Demoralized Majority

1) In the Bleak Mid-Future

Let's say that you worked for a company whose internal newsletter ran an article with the headline: "Do our employees still have a place in the business?" and then went on to suggest several "questions" to ponder before we rushed to say "No". If you think that this might make you a little nervous about your future in the company then you might begin to get a sense of the mood of the parish clergy who were greeted with exactly this situation when they read the March 1997 edition of the Anglican Journal. The editorial was entitled "Do clergy still have a role in the church?". While the editor made some excellent points, the very fact that the question was raised in the first place would inevitably be seen as a serious threat to a group that has sometimes thought and acted as if it and the Church were synonymous.

The fact that these editorial musings arose out of a clergy conference is significant. If one way in which the Church is facing the crisis is to pass responsibility down to the local level, another is to try to prepare its clergy for the trauma ahead. Not having a solution to the situation, the leadership is at least attempting to develop a strategy for survival. The typical clergy conference brings in an expert of some sort who makes it clear to the clergy that the coming major decline in church membership will impact severely upon their careers.

The Church of the future will obviously have less full-time clergy because it will only be about half the present size. In fact, the clergy are being encouraged to become "bi-vocational". The expectation is that many will only be able to have a part-time position in the Church and will need a second job if they hope to pull in an adequate income. Furthermore, greater emphasis will be placed on the role of non-stipendiary clergy. This is a very hard message for the current clergy community to hear. To have to think about a second "vocation" in mid-career is extremely traumatic to those so used to a high degree of job security and whose skills are not as portable as some others.

2) Whatever Happened to "The Ministry"?

Beyond even this it is becoming all too clear that the nature of the job itself, even for those few who might remain in full-time positions, will have to change significantly. The current crop of clergy received its calling and training within the old system and has learned to function within its various structures and expectations. Basically clergy were seen as the persons in the Church who did "the ministry". To discover that they are now to become those who train the laity for ministry is not necessarily welcome news. At the very least it raises questions about their own calling and their ability to take on new tasks for which they may have neither appropriate gifts nor training.

All this is to say that the reality of the unacknowledged crisis is beginning to take its toll within the clergy of the Anglican Church of Canada. Being on the frontlines, they know very well that the Church is in serious trouble and that they are going to take the brunt of the inevitable difficulties ahead. Discontentment has become one of the burdens of office. Younger clergy wonder if there will be a place for them at all while older clergy find themselves unattractive to parishes desperate to attract younger people back to church. What was formerly a pastoral relationship between the bishop and his clergy is descending into the vortex of employee - employer relationships including the inevitable involvement of lawsuits and lawyers.

3) Going Down in Flames

When we add to this the long list of problems already facing the profession as a whole, the sense of crisis increases almost to the breaking point. A catalogue would include marriage breakdown, underpayment, a perceived loss of power vis a vis the bishops, lack of collegiality, multiplication of meetings, little measurable career success, loss of prestige in the community, an unresponsive bureaucracy, unending conflict, an uncertain message, workaholism, too many hours, changed role expectations, lack of supervision or accountability, inadequate training, unending parish and diocesan budget pressures, and, finally...burnout. The continuing difficulties of the Church in dealing with incompetence or in restoring those who require rehabilitation only completes the disturbing picture.

4) Conclusion: I Can't Get No Satisfaction

None of this is imply that Anglican clergy are worse off than many other professionals or that there are no compensating factors which can make their calling rich and rewarding. However it is very difficult to imagine a group of "employees" more dissatisfied with their current job experience that the clergy of the Anglican Church of Canada. Here I speak from the inside, as one who has been to many clergy conferences, engaged in countless conversations and observed the situation first hand. It is thoroughly demoralizing. Conditions are well into the danger zone. Ask the bishops! They are so busy trying to put out the "fires" resulting from all this stress that they have almost no time for their traditional role of chief pastor and teacher.

This is not the way it is supposed to be!

(c) The Mood in the House of Laity: Bewitched, Bothered and Bewildered

Bewitched, bothered and bewildered. This is the best way I can think of to describe the current disposition of the laity of the ACC. They too, perhaps more profoundly than the other "houses", are feeling the effects of the crisis that no one dares to name. It should be understood that what follows hardly applies to all of the laity but it does, I would argue, fit the general pattern of the feeling within this segment of the Church.

1) Bewitched

"Bewitched", because although they have been involved in the decision-making processes of the Church for some time they still appear to be under the spell of the clergy. Some high profile lay leaders still seem to believe the clergy have a special kind of knowledge, language and spiritual power which sets them "above" the common folk. This unfortunate situation arises largely from the fact that while the laity have been invited to a fuller participation in the life of the Church they remain woefully unprepared for this role. Typically, Anglican lay persons have received only a perfunctory religious education in their Church and thus when it comes to dealing with the theological issues at the heart of Christian life they are at a severe disadvantage. On the one side we have persons with graduate degrees in theology while on the other we have persons who have graduated from Sunday School. No wonder the latter defer to the former! It is only natural. It is also regrettable.

2) Bothered

"Bothered", because in a matter of a single generation they have seen their Church lose much of its familiar shape, especially in terms of its identifying liturgy, the Book of Common Prayer. This was not their doing. They went along with these changes, especially the "imposition" (as many justifiably feel) of the Book of Alternative Services, primarily because they accepted the judgment of the clergy-leadership that they were necessary in order to "make the Church relevant to the current generation". Instead, the Church has gone from being a key part of the "Canadian establishment" to being almost ignored by the wider culture and only an also-ran within the Christian community. Anglican laity have lost their beloved way of worship and it has profited them nothing. At least this is the way that many seem to see it. Now they exist in an institution which is threatened on every side as well as from within. Nothing seems to be working properly. Many of those who have not simply left continue to have a great smoldering anger and sense of betrayal. This ugly truth is on display all too often in the "Letters to the Editor" of the Anglican Journal. It is truly distressing to see such open wounds. But they are real and they are us.

3) Bewildered

"Bewildered", because they have little idea what has happened to their Church or what to do in order to reform or renew it. Too many of the familiar landmarks on their ecclesiastical landscape have been moved or taken away altogether. The old certainties of their faith are routinely denied or reinterpreted by prominent members of their leadership. So many words are spoken but no one seems to know what is being said. The Church seems more like Babel with its confusion of tongues than Pentecost where each one hears the Word clearly in his own language. Each new rector seems to have his or her own differing perspective on the faith once delivered to the saints. Visiting in a different parish, even the one next door, often now involves going into an alien world. Meanwhile, those in positions of responsibility remain strangely silent in the face of obvious crisis. What is going on?

(d) Conclusion: Diagnosis Confirmed

All three "houses" within the Anglican Church of Canada are suffering from a severe form of the plague. It is simply impossible to deny that this is true.

In ancient times people had a variety of fanciful explanations as to what caused the plague or how it spread on its deadly course from house to house and so through the population. Because of their ignorance, they were unable to protect themselves and avoid its devastating effect.

It is to be hoped that the analysis which now follows will be closer to the truth than these antiquated tales and will prove more helpful in arresting the scourge now inflicting itself upon us all.

(iv) Yes, Virginia, There is a Crisis

This has been a difficult chapter. Reality can be hard to take. The Anglican Church of Canada is in deep crisis. The symptoms of membership loss, recruitment difficulties, declining income, disorder, elitism along with general discouragement and confusion all point in the same direction. This cannot be denied. But, as I said in the Introduction, facing the truth is the first step on the road to recovery. Not an easy step, but the first step.

The next step is to understand how we got into such a mess in the first place.

CHAPTER THREE

How We Got Here From There

By the grace God has given me, I laid a foundation as an expert builder, and someone else is building on it. But each one should be careful how he builds. For no one can lay any foundation other than the one already laid, which is Jesus Christ. If any man builds on this foundation using gold, silver, costly stones, wood, hay or straw, his work will be shown for what it is, because the Day will bring it to light. (I Corinthians 3:10-13)

(i) Where Did It Come From?: The Rise of the Liberal Religion

(a) Introduction: A Reasonable Explanation

How did we manage to get into this situation? Let us trace the ideas and events which have made significant contributions to the current crisis in the Anglican Church of Canada. While this book makes no claim to be scholarly, it nevertheless represents a genuine effort to grapple with the reality of our past. Although I must take responsibility for what I have written, it is important to stress that many in the Church share the general point of view here expressed. If it needs correction it is urgent that it be done quickly in order to spare us from unnecessary conflict and division. We can only be brought closer together by the truth and it is in the give and take of discussion (or argument!) that illusions will dissolve and truth will emerge. However, none of this should be taken as implying a lack of confidence in the fundamental correctness of what I have to say.

(b) Two Does Not Go Into One

I shall argue that, in reality, our major problems are caused or made worse by the introduction of "liberalism" into the life of our denomination. Until this situation is dealt with, the other problems, and there are many, cannot be effectively resolved. I shall demonstrate that liberalism is not the classical Christianity of our mothers and fathers of the last two thousand years. It is in fact another religion altogether and actually stands opposed to classical Christianity on almost every important theological issue. *Our crisis exists largely, but not exclusively, because these two incompatible and opposed religions, each with its own vision and purpose, co-exist in our church. This is our fundamental problem. It has led to a terrible kind of institutional paralysis. No organization can long continue in such a state of division.*

In order to better grasp this truth it is necessary to see it in historical perspective. In this manner it is easier to see that what has happened in the Church is not merely the natural development of Anglicanism's famous "comprehensiveness". Rather something fundamental has changed, bringing us into a situation entirely without precedent. As such, old solutions will simply not do. Something more will be needed.

(c) As It Was In the Beginning

1) Essentially Together

From its very origins in the sixteenth century, the Church of England (and its daughter churches in other countries) has been relatively tolerant of a variety of theological perspectives. It is beyond the scope of this treatise to outline the reasons for this tolerance but there is no dispute about its reality. However, something does need to be said about the general *nature* of this tolerance. Until recently it has been a tolerance within certain well-understood limits and which presumed a core of basic Christian truth shared within the one holy catholic church ("catholic" in the sense of "universal", containing all the branches of Christ's scattered flock).

This attitude was perhaps best expressed by the seventeenth century cleric Richard Baxter to whom is credited the famous dictum: "In essentials, unity; in non-essentials, liberty; and in all things, charity" (*Anglican Essentials,* p. 11). By following this in a kind of informal fashion over the years, the Anglican community has been able to hold an amazing diversity of views within its bosom while retaining a significant degree of cohesion. The latter, strained almost to the breaking point at several moments in its history, has nevertheless managed to hold. At least until now.

2) The "Articles" of Our Belief

What has held it together has been a more or less universal acceptance of what *constitutes* those "essentials", the common ground upon which we stand. Historically this was the specific function of the famous "Thirty-Nine Articles" that appear at the end of the Book of Common Prayer (pp. 698-714). Here we find what used to be the basic doctrines of the Anglican faith. Generations of clergy had to agree to them as part of the ordination process "...for the avoiding of diversities of opinions and for the establishing of consent touching true religion." This quotation is from the Title Page that used to precede the Articles (prior to 1962) along with King Charles the First's "Royal Declaration" of 1628. In the latter the king recognized that there was indeed some leeway of interpretation of the Articles but he took care to guard their centrality, insisting that all clergymen

> ...agree in the true, usual, literal meaning of the said Articles; and that even in those curious points, in which the present differences lie, men of all sorts take the Articles of the Church of England to be for them: which is an argument...that none of them intend any desertion of the Articles established.
>
> ...no man hereafter shall either print, or preach, to draw the Article aside in any way, but shall submit to it in the plain and full meaning thereof: and shall not put his own sense or comment to be the meaning of the Article, but shall take it in the literal and grammatical sense.
>
> ...if any publick Reader in either of Our Universities, or any Head or Master of a College, or any other person respectively in either of them, shall affix any new sense to any Article, or shall publickly read, determine, or hold any publick Disputation or suffer any such to be held ...he, or they the Offenders, shall be liable to Our displeasure, and the Church's censure...(BCP [1918 ed.], p. 658)

So much for authentic Anglican tolerance! In practice this seemed to result in a wide enough variety of opinion within these parameters. Even at the height of his fierce battle with anglo-catholicism, the controversial nineteenth century evangelical Bishop of Liverpool, J. C. Ryle was able to say:

> I have always allowed, and do allow, that our Church is largely comprehensive, and that there is room for honest High, honest Low, and honest Broad Churchmen within her pale...But I firmly maintain that the comprehensiveness of the Church has limits, and that those limits are the Thirty-nine Articles and the Prayer-book. (*Principles for Churchmen*, p. 71)

Historically, then, the Anglican Church has always known both that it had borders and where those borders were. It is now necessary to ask what enabled it to mark out such clear boundaries in the first place. When we have discovered these foundations and what has happened to them, then we will understand why there is such confusion in the contemporary Church and perhaps even find a way forward through the all the noise.

(3) Underneath the Bible

Another historical event can serve to shed some light on the true roots of our commonality as Anglicans. At the same time that Ryle was concerning himself with what now seem to be quaint and insignificant divisions within the Church of England, there was a gathering sense of optimism regarding the possibility of Christian reunification. In reflecting on these matters during the Lambeth Conference of 1888 the bishops of the Church carefully outlined another, more minimal, list of Christian "essentials" upon which any hope for a reunified Christendom must rest. This became known as the "Lambeth Quadrilateral" and it is worth quoting in full at this point.

> (a) The Holy Scriptures of the Old and New Testaments, as "containing all things necessary to salvation," and as being the rule and ultimate standard of faith.
>
> (b) The Apostle's Creed, as the Baptismal Symbol; and the Nicene Creed, as the sufficient statement of the Christian faith.
>
> (c) The two Sacraments,- Baptism and the Supper of the Lord, - ministered with the unfailing use of Christ's words of institution and of the elements ordained by Him.
>
> (d) The Historic Episcopate, locally adapted in the methods of its administration to the various needs of the nations and peoples called of God into the unity of his Church. (Episcopal Book of Common Prayer, p. 877-8)

There are a number of things that should be noted about this important document. First of all there is, in the first clause, an inherent expression of the final authority of the Bible over the Church. Many Anglicans have been taught that authority in Anglican theology is seen as a three-legged stool of Scripture, reason and tradition. To the extent that this metaphor implies the equivalence of these three sources it is simply wrong. It is better to say that Anglicans recognize the importance of reason and tradition in seeking to understand what it is that Scripture is saying. Even more important, we are never to put reason or tradition *over* Scripture. It is the ultimate authority and this is what we see all the bishops of the Church affirming when they insist on this clause.

The second thing to meditate upon is that it was the *bishops* who issued this Quadrilateral. They took the initiative and provided significant leadership not only to those within the Anglican fold but also to the whole of the Christian church. Today they are, at least in Canada, largely silent in the face of a Church in crisis. Not only are they silent, they give every appearance of urging silence on the rest of the Church as well. When others, out of a sense of frustration and urgency, have gathered themselves together outside the official structures of the Church in an attempt to offer a contemporary list of "essentials" for consideration they have received a very cool reception from many in official positions of leadership. It seems that the very idea of insisting on a number of "essentials", whatever those are conceived to be, is just not on. Needless to say this represents a radical change from the situation at the turn of the century.

The third thing is to observe that J.C. Ryle's insistence on the Thirty-nine Articles and the Prayer Book does not contradict what the bishops say about the position of the Bible in the Church. After all, these two standards maintain the same attitude toward Scriptural authority expressed by the Quadrilateral. Indeed, until recently, our Church has spoken with one voice on this subject. The position of the Bible was the central theological issue underlying the English Reformation (as it was in other parts of Europe). And it is not just Anglicans who have always seen the Bible as the ultimate standard of faith. It is but the natural outgrowth of catholic Christianity's conviction about the nature of the Holy Scriptures.

All Christendom held that the Scriptures are the very Word of God written and are without error in all that they affirm. This was the view of Our Lord, the Apostles and early church, the Fathers, St. Augustine, St. Thomas Aquinas, Luther, Calvin, Thomas Cramner and all the English Reformers, Richard Hooker (the quintessential Anglican theologian) and all the Anglican "divines". While it is true that this "doctrine" has never been officially adopted by the Anglican Church it is the unspoken but necessary assumption that runs through the whole foundation of its theological structure.

Until quite recently, there was simply no serious debate or division on this issue in the whole history of the Christian faith. The only question was not about the nature of the Bible but about whether or not its authority was superseded in some way by that of the Church. On this question, as we have seen, Anglicanism has always said that the Church is under the Scriptures and not vice versa. This was re-affirmed as recently as the Lambeth Conference of 1958.

4) One Holy, Catholic and Biblical Church

(A) Biblical Authority and Catholic Faith

So far I have sought to argue that Anglicanism has historically seen its famous tolerance limited by the acceptance of common set of core doctrines. These have always included an explicit affirmation of the final authority of the Scriptures as well as an implicit affirmation of the universal Christian conviction that these Scriptures were the Word of God written and thus absolutely reliable. *It is critical to recognize that all these central doctrines of the Christian church, all of the basic elements of its message, its very conception of God and what he has done in Christ for the salvation of humanity were developed out of and depend upon this attitude to the Bible. Wherever it has held sway these same central doctrines have been held by every variation within what we have come to call the Church catholic (i.e., universal).* This is not to say that the myriad and unfortunate divisions within the church have always been over relatively peripheral issues. However, when the divisions have been over core doctrine it is because one side or the other (or both!) have placed some other authority over Scripture.

While I believe that what I have said is simply a matter of logic and historical fact there will be many who will dispute it on the grounds of its being overly simplistic (and probably on other grounds too!). Let me be clear. I am not claiming that holding the classical understanding of the nature and authority of Holy Scripture automatically or easily results in the emergence of the central doctrines of the orthodox Christian faith. This is ultimately the work of the Holy Spirit who both inspired the Scriptures in the first place and continues to witness to their truth and meaning in each generation. But when the guiding principle of theological reasoning is rooted in the classical view of Scripture at the end of the day it will produce the fundamental beliefs shared by all catholic Christians.

(B) Reality Check: The Evangelical Fellowship of Canada

In order to both illustrate and buttress my argument I would direct my reader's attention to the Evangelical Fellowship of Canada as a kind of living proof. Here we have a contemporary Christian organization which joins together what at first appears to be a bewildering variety of denominations, congregations and individuals, all of whom are committed to just the kind of Biblical authority under discussion.

While it is true that the denominations in the Fellowship remain mutually exclusive and differ considerably from one another on a number of doctrinal matters they all at the same time share a deep commitment to the central doctrines of classical orthodox Christianity. They are all Trinitarians, they all accept the pre-incarnate divinity of Our Lord, they all preach the atoning sacrifice of Jesus' death on the Cross and they all proclaim his bodily resurrection from the dead. All of them. Indeed, all subscribe to the Fellowship's "Statement of Faith" which corresponds remarkably to the core of essentials which were once considered necessary for Anglicans and all catholic Christians.

Thus a commitment to the classical concept of Biblical authority is inevitably linked to a similar commitment to the core doctrines of classical orthodoxy. This can be observed both in history and in contemporary Christian life. Those who believe that such a commitment to Biblical authority is inadequate to produce anything but utter doctrinal confusion are simply in error. It has, in actual fact, produced remarkable doctrinal unity. Admittedly, this unity does not extend itself over the whole range of doctrine and is not (yet) expressed in organizational unity. Denominations and movements continue to exhibit a distressing tendency to fragment even while admitting that they continue to share the basic faith with those from whom they are distancing themselves. Many still seem unwilling to make a proper distinction between what is of primary importance and what is secondary.

Perhaps it is not too arrogant suggest that a good dose of authentic Anglican tolerance (a la Richard Baxter) might help provide the perspective necessary to keep us all more fully in the family. This could be part of the witness of a reformed and renewed Anglicanism to the whole body of Christ. That would bring us closer to the fulfillment of the famous Anglican plea that "... all they that do confess thy holy Name may agree in the truth of thy holy Word, and live in unity and godly love" (BCP, p. 75). This intercession, by the way, is a wonderfully compact expression of the authentic Anglican understanding that Christian unity is based upon agreement about the teaching of Holy Scripture, which is the truth. The Collect for Saint Simon and Saint Jude, reflecting the same attitude, forms an appropriate end to this section:

> O Almighty God, who has built thy Church upon the foundation of the Apostles and Prophets, Jesus Christ himself being the head corner-stone: Grant us so to be *joined together in unity of spirit by their doctrine*, that we may be made an holy temple acceptable unto thee; through Jesus Christ our Lord. *Amen.* (My italics)

5) Guarding the Truth

(A) Introduction: The "Conservative Principle"

Not only is the above prayer an appropriate end to the above discussion but it also leads us into a consideration of another aspect of the classical Anglican attitude to the Scriptures. If one is convinced that the

Bible, as the Word of God written, is both absolutely trustworthy and the final authority in matters of Christian belief, one is also necessarily committed to what might be called the "conservative principle": whatever the Bible teaches is to remain unaltered. It is a deposit of truth which is to be guarded and passed on from one generation of believers to the next. We are to remain loyal to its message because it is the message of authentic Christianity.

(B) It Is Written

This implication deriving from the nature of classical Biblical authority is reinforced by the actual teaching that we find in the Scriptures themselves. Again and again the early church is exhorted to not depart from what it has been taught. At one point St. Paul says that "even if we or an angel from heaven should preach a gospel other than the one we preached to you, let him be eternally condemned." (Gal. 1:8). There is also a dire warning at the end of the book of Revelation which could apply to the whole of the Bible:

> I warn everyone who hears the words of the prophecy of this book. If anyone adds anything to them, God will add to him the plagues described in this book. And if anyone takes words away from this book of prophecy, God will take away from him his share in the tree of life and in the holy city... (Rev. 22:18,19.

(C) Solemnly Declared

Just as Anglicanism has affirmed its commitment to the classical view of Scripture, so also has it expressed its desire to follow the conservative principle. For example, in the Supplementary Instruction the Confirmation from the Book of Common Prayer the candidate is asked, "Why is (the Church) called Apostolic?" and the answer is "Because it receive its divine mission from Christ through his Apostles, and *continues in their doctrine and fellowship*" (p. 553). In that same Instruction we are told that the Church teaches that "The Bible records the Word of God ...and nothing may be taught in the Church as necessary to salvation unless it be concluded or proved therefrom." (p. 554-5)

At one time in the Canadian church our Bishops explicitly committed themselves to this same view of the Bible and accepted the responsibility to "...be ready, with all faithful diligence, to banish and drive away all erroneous and strange doctrine *contrary to God's Word*; and both privately and openly to call upon others to do the same." (BCP, p. 663) While this latter commitment is omitted by the Book of Alternative Services the new Bishop does declare "the holy scriptures of the Old and New Testaments to be the word of God, and to contain all things necessary to salvation;" and promises to "...be faithful in prayer, and in the study of holy scripture..." in order to "...have the mind of Christ...". He also accepts the responsibility to "...guard the faith.." of the Church (pp. 635-7) which suggests that the faith is a given, an inheritance which cannot be altered.

Perhaps the most spectacular commitment to this position was made by the Bishops, clergy and laity of the very first General Synod of the Anglican Church of Canada in 1893. It is contained in the famous "Solemn Declaration" now included at the front of the Book of Common Prayer (p. vii). As the founding document of the denomination it bears careful consideration. This is especially true because those who brought the ACC into being clearly saw themselves as committing the denomination to this view for all posterity. It is worth quoting at this point:

> We declare this Church to be, and desire that it shall continue, in full communion with the Church of England throughout the world, as an integral portion of the One Body of Christ composed of Churches which...hold the One Faith revealed in Holy Writ, and defined in the Creeds...; receive the same Canonical Scriptures of the Old and New Testaments, as containing all things necessary to salvation; teach the same Word of God...
>
> And we are determined by the help of God to hold and maintain the Doctrine, Sacraments and Discipline of Christ as the Lord hath commanded in his Holy Word, and as the Church of England hath received and set forth the same in The Book of Common Prayer...; and in the Thirty-nine Articles of Religion; and to transmit the same unimpaired to our posterity.

This commitment has never been revoked. In fact, the Declaration is given prominent place in the last revision of the Book of Common Prayer in 1959. It is preceded in that Book only by "The Preface to the Canadian Revision of 1918 Altered in 1959" which contains the following forceful statements which clearly reveal the mind of the revisers:

> In the years of preparation and study, the principles which governed those who first gave the Church its Book of Common Prayer have been constantly borne in mind. The aim throughout has been to set forth an order which ...is agreeable with Holy Scripture and with the usage of the primitive Church. *And always there has been the understanding that no alterations should be made which would involve or imply any change of doctrine of the Church as set forth in the Book of Common Prayer...*
>
> When the Bishops, Clergy, and Laity of the Church in Canada assembled for the first General Synod in 1893, they made a Solemn Declaration of the faith in which they met together. *It is in that faith that this Book of Common Prayer is offered to the Church...*(p. vii)

6) Conclusion: Keeping To the Way

Thus it is fair to conclude that up until 1960 or so the Anglican Church of Canada officially continued to conform to the pattern established from the beginning. It saw itself committed to the supreme authority of Holy Scripture and to the "conservative principle" wherein the apostolic faith was to be retained, proclaimed and guarded by the Church. For generations the revision of the liturgy had been conducted within this framework and understanding. This was the Anglican way.

(d) Something New This Way Comes

1) What Meaneth This Book?

Based on what has been said so far one might be excused for assuming that when the ACC next faced calls for liturgical revision in the late seventies, a mere twenty years later, a similar set of principles would guide the process. However, one glance at the resulting Book of Alternative Services, produced in 1985, is enough to convince anyone that in many ways it is radically discontinuous with any previous revision.

While most of its differences may have more to do with the form of worship rather than any substantive change in belief, such change is certainly not absent. Indeed, for the first time in Anglican history the authors of a new liturgy stated a desire to distance themselves from central aspects of the basic theology expressed in the Book of Common Prayer (BAS pp. 178-9). Instead of committing themselves to "...hold and maintain the Doctrine...as the Church of England hath received and set forth the same in the Book of Common Prayer..." they attempted to return to the use of the more "fluid images" which they perceived in "the biblical material", certain ancient liturgies and patristic theologies. Given this attempt to "go back" beyond the Reformation, it seems odd, at first glance, that in the "Introduction" they stress the vast changes in the world since the sixteenth century which necessitate this new approach. With all this emphasis on "difference" it comes as no surprise that the BAS makes no effort to remind Anglicans of the *Solemn Declaration* or of the *Preface* which grace the front of the Book of Common Prayer.

Whatever the merits of these changes, for our purposes it is important only to note that they represent a significant new departure for the Anglican Church of Canada. For over four centuries the Church had been following one pattern of liturgical revision and then suddenly, out of the blue, it turned its back on its past and veered off in a completely new direction. As we have already seen, a mere fifteen years after adopting these new principles the pace and magnitude of liturgical change continues to grow and are now seriously threatening our sense of unity and even of what it means to be an Anglican

Christian. For good or bad, the face of the Church has been deeply altered. It also seems like it will be perpetually under the knife as the plastic surgeons of liturgical revision find themselves fully employed.

While it must be acknowledged that the life of the Church consists in much more than its liturgy, there can also be no doubt that they are closely connected. Thus the pattern of change we have observed represents even more profound changes beneath the surface. Clearly something very dramatic has happened within the wider life of the Church to bring about the changes in the liturgy. How could an institution, after 450 years of steady development in one direction suddenly find itself going in another one altogether? How could a Church which was the very embodiment of stuffy uniformity for centuries become a laboratory for constant change within less than a generation? Understanding the answer to these questions will go a long way towards clearing up a lot of our confusion and may even help point the way forward out of our present crisis.

2) Another "Quiet Revolution"

In many ways what has happened to the Anglican Church of Canada can be compared to the so-called "Quiet Revolution" which has taken place in the Province of Quebec. For generations Quebec appeared to be a solidly monolithic society. The Roman Catholic Church was firmly in control of the culture. Religion permeated every aspect of the civilization, dominating almost every institution, including education and politics. But, behind the scenes and unnoticed by many, a "quiet revolution" was taking place. Many Quebecers, especially among the intellectual elite, were abandoning the faith of their fathers and most of what it represented in favour of a secular nationalism. Even as recently as thirty years ago a casual observer could be excused for thinking that all was as it had been. Quebec gave every appearance of still being an old world Catholic society. But behind the facade almost everything had changed. The new faith had largely supplanted the old and could not be contained within the confines of the old institutions which had unwittingly nourished it. The revolution, when it finally erupted in the early seventies, left a shriveled, shattered and dispirited Roman Catholic community in its wake. It had lost Quebec almost overnight.

So it was in the Anglican Church of Canada. Although it presented an official traditional/orthodox face to the world, momentous changes were taking place behind the scenes. For over a hundred years increasing numbers within its ruling elite had been educated in an approach to religion that was rooted in a rejection of the basic assumptions that had stood behind the Christian theological framework for almost two millennia. Inevitably many came to accept this new way of thinking and as a result distanced themselves from the traditional understanding of the Faith. For a variety of reasons, instead of simply leaving the Church as one might expect (now that they no longer accepted its official teaching), they saw themselves as merely *re-interpreting* the Faith in ways acceptable to "modern man". This resulted in a great deal of misunderstanding within the denomination because they continued to use the language of Faith but actually meant something entirely different by the old familiar words. In this context there was (and continues to be) a certain amount of psychological pressure to be less than open about one's opposition to official doctrinal positions.

Given also the enormous self-confidence of official Anglicanism (shared by the whole church of that age) and its tradition of tolerating differing theological views, it hardly seems surprising that little was done to confront these developments. More and more of the positions of power fell into the hands of those of the newer persuasion. Certainly by the late 1970's (and arguably much earlier than that) this new understanding had reached a kind of "critical mass" within the leadership allowing its agenda to go increasingly mainstream. What might seem like a huge gap between the affirmation of traditional Anglicanism in 1959 and a self-conscious departure from that tradition in 1985 was really the logical outworking out of a process that had been going on for several generations. The "quiet revolution" was over. It was going to get real noisy, real fast.

What I have just described is a kind of "inner history" of the Anglican Church over the last hundred years and is necessarily full of generalities and sweeping statements. Nevertheless I am convinced that the picture painted is broadly true and can be verified by anyone who cares to investigate. In fact, I hope that this task will be taken up by professional church historians in order to provide us with a fuller picture. As far as I know there has been no attempt to write this kind of history of the Anglican Church of Canada.

3) A Brave New Worldview

(A) Humanity Comes Of Age

In order to understand these developments more fully it is necessary to explore the nature of this "new way of thinking" that has been introduced into the life of the Church. The assumptions underlying the message and mission of the catholic church had to do with the nature and authority of the Bible as God's word written. Simply put, the church had always accepted the truth and accuracy of the Bible. If it claimed something had happened in a certain way then that was in fact the way it happened. If it claimed something to be true then it was true. For example, the Gospels clearly state that Our Lord was born of a virgin mother and therefore this fact was never seriously disputed within the church. Obviously this acceptance of the truth of Scripture took place within a worldview that was open to the possibility of the miraculous.

The entire theological structure of the catholic church was erected upon this foundation.

With the arrival of the so-called "Enlightenment" or "Age of Reason" in the 17th century this worldview came into serious question. Man had become the measure of all things. Human reason became the new authority and the rise of science with its many spectacular successes lent a great air of optimism to this turn in our intellectual history. The suffocating shrouds of "authority" and "tradition" were cast aside and man stood to his full height and surveyed his own domain. One of the dominating philosophies that developed in this atmosphere was "empiricism" which held that knowledge could only be derived from sense experience. One of its implications was that, because we do not experience miracles in our day-to-day lives, they do not in fact happen. This view corresponded to the newly emerging theory that nature functions according to certain unbreakable "laws". Since a miracle (like a virgin giving birth) would involve the breaking of one of these laws it was automatically excluded from the realm of possibility. It just couldn't happen.

While this brief account is hardly adequate to the task, it can serve to highlight the basic pattern of our intellectual history. All that remains to be pointed out is that the new views came quickly to dominate the intellectual establishment of the Western world. In fact it is only in the very recent past that such assumptions and theories have come under serious question, especially with the rise of the "new" physics. But for generations it was the faith that guided thinkers in our culture.

It is impossible to exaggerate the dimensions of the threat that these developments posed to the traditional/orthodox version of the Christian faith. If these new views were true then the church had been misreading the Bible for over 1500 years. It would mean that its understanding of who Jesus actually was would have to be radically altered, if not abandoned altogether. No longer could he be born of a virgin, heal the sick, control natural elements, know the future, rise bodily from the dead nor rise up into heaven on a cloud as the Scriptures plainly taught. This in turn cast grave doubt on the Bible as the utterly reliable Word of God. And, as I have stressed, this assumption underpinned the whole Christian theological enterprise.

While the vast majority within the church simply continued, with varying degrees of tension, to hold to the old view of the Scriptures for a number of generations, there was an increasing number within her ranks who more or less came to accept the new one. And thus "liberalism" was born. Fundamentally, it involves the rejection of the traditional/orthodox assumptions regarding the nature and authority of Scripture. Desiring the right to be free to go wherever Reason and Conscience should lead, it seeks to encourage the church to change its positions in a progressive direction in order to meet the changed conditions in which it finds itself. Once severed from those assumptions that underlay the traditional shape of the faith, liberalism has produced a bewildering variety of alternative visions of Christianity. This is more than a little curious given the promise inherent in adopting a "scientific" methodology. One would think that having left behind the wrong methodology for the right one there would have been assured results. The opposite seems to be true. In fact it is a commonplace observation that each generation of liberals has tended to advocate versions of the faith that on examination prove to be little more than Christianized expressions of the secular philosophy of their day.

(B) Looking For the "Real" Jesus

In line with this new approach, many sought to apply the principles of the new "historical criticism" to the Biblical record in an attempt to uncover the "Jesus of history". It was assumed that the latter would emerge from the layers of legend and misunderstanding which had obscured him in the Bible. Behind this assumption was another: the "real" Jesus, the Jesus of history, would be a man to whom we would be drawn and who would command our allegiance. If we could just get back to him and the "pure" Christianity that he taught we would be in touch with the unadulterated essence of the Faith. In a way this was a version of the "conservative principle", the difference being that the church had always taught that the Jesus of history *was* the Jesus of the Bible and thus the aim was to get back to the Bible. Now the aim was, and still is, to get back to the Jesus who lay *behind* the Bible.

The 18th and 19th centuries produced what came to be known as the "Quest of the Historical Jesus". A number of "lives" of Jesus were written from the new perspective, each of them differing considerably from the other. This whole effort collapsed around the beginning of our century after Albert Schwietzer astutely pointed out that each of these "real" Jesuses was made in the image of the author who tried to reconstruct him. For a time this realization seemed to encourage a return to "biblical theology" but this did not endure. Instead there arose a very influential stream of thought that went the other way entirely and insisted that the unknowable Jesus of history was irrelevant to faith after all. Although this was a logical conclusion, given the inability of scholars actually to produce the historical Jesus, this theory was quickly judged to be in conflict with the historical nature of Christianity. Therefore in the early 1950's scholarship once again set off in another "Quest of the Historical Jesus". He has continued to prove extremely elusive.

This fact came clearly to the surface with the recent television programs, newspaper articles and magazine covers focused on the "Jesus Seminar". (c.f. "Can the New Jesus Save Us?" by C. Stephen Evans, *Books and Culture,* November/December 1995, pp. 3-8) This is one of the few times that mainstream scholarship has surfaced in the popular media and it attracted a fair amount of attention. It brought together a large number of

New Testament scholars in an attempt to decide whether or not Jesus actually said the things the Bible reports him as saying. Each scholar voted on each "saying" by dropping a coloured bead into a box. If he thought that Jesus probably did say it or something like it he would use a red bead, while if he thought the Lord probably never said it or anything like it he would use a black one. Other colours stood for shades of probability in between. The result of the vote indicated that this particular group of scholars thought that only 18 percent of what the Bible attributes to Jesus was actually said by him.

While such a conclusion may seem shocking to the average lay person, at least it gives us a solid basis for our understanding of the real Jesus of history. Or does it? On closer inspection it is easy to see that it does no such thing. First of all it is important to realize that not all of the scholars *agreed* on the authenticity of this 18 percent. Those were only the sayings which at least a simple majority of the scholars thought deserved a red bead. In other words, those sayings that made the grade might only be accepted as authentic by just over half of those voting. Those scholars who disagreed with the majority did not change their minds because they lost the vote! In spite of the impression that the Jesus Seminar manages to convey, its participants remain divided about even the tiny percentage judged to be really from Jesus himself.

To add further to the uncertainty of these results we also need to recognize that if a different group of scholars with a different set of assumptions at a different moment in history had participated in the Jesus Seminar the results would have been different as well. A modern Albert Schwietzer might also observe that the Jesus which emerges from this endeavour manages to sound remarkably like what many of us would like him to sound.

(C) Conclusion: Free-Falling Apart

My point here is that the democratic procedure of the Jesus Seminar does not and indeed cannot render any truly reliable results. The same is true of all the methodologies of liberalism. Once liberated from having to accept *all* of Jesus' sayings as authentic (the traditional/orthodox view, the view of the "church"), scholars are free to pick and choose according to whatever criteria they deem helpful. They are obviously guided in their judgments by their own philosophical and ideological presumptions. Furthermore, when one actually reads the efforts of these scholars one discovers that they are constantly building hypothesis upon hypothesis upon hypothesis. And, like building a house of cards, whatever they construct is regularly collapsing and being rebuilt. The result is something near chaos. The world of modern biblical scholarship is riddled by a bewildering variety of ideas, trends, schools of thought, nationalities, cultures, languages, Churches, philosophies, gurus, jealousies and rivalries. Just like any other human endeavour.

What we therefore discover is that no one picture of the teachings of Jesus emerges from the efforts of modern scholarship. There are only pictures. Using the same general methodology, scholars have come to opposite conclusions. For example, some suggest that Jesus was a kind of wandering Greek philosopher who challenged the prevailing social and cultural assumptions of his day while others highlight the more or less conventional Jewishness of who he was. Some see Jesus preaching that the end of the world is still in the near future, while others have him stressing the present reality of God's kingdom. Some hold that only the *actions* of Jesus can be known. Others claim the opposite, that only his *sayings* can be known. Some see him as uninterested in the politics of the day while to others he was advocating a revolution against Roman oppression. The only sure conclusion we can draw is that this methodology produces no sure conclusions!

Not long ago many liberals, having turned aside from supernaturalism, reinterpreted the Christian language of spirituality in terms of modern secular psychology. Nowadays, in a startling departure, but again following the secular culture, many liberals have embraced New Age spirituality. This can be described as a kind of generic supernaturalism. Angels, spirits, shamans, goddesses and witches are now being taken seriously and eagerly incorporated into "Christian" spirituality and worship. At the turn of the century liberals were loudly proclaiming "The Fatherhood of God and the Brotherhood of Man". Now, in an almost complete reversal, one hears calls for "The Motherhood of God and the Sisterhood of Women"!

Indeed, this last observation leads to another. The latest theological trend is to echo the radical feminist agenda which has made itself felt in the "politically correct" movement which has swept across many of our secular university campuses. The same phenomenon is now arriving with a vengeance at our seminaries. The efforts of this kind of feminist theology to remake the Church in its own image are nothing short of breathtaking. It is also increasingly straightforward about it. Because it is the latest thing it is important that we gain some understanding of what direction it is going. The best way to do this is to examine the conference called "Re-Imagining" which took place in 1993. While this cannot be done in any detail in this paper, it is important to realize that it took place under the auspices of the World Council of Churches' initiative "The Ecumenical Decade: Churches in Solidarity with Women, 1988-98" and received funding from a number of mainline denominations.

For our purposes we need only pay heed to the comments of Kwok Pui-Lan, a professor of theology at Episcopal Divinity School in Cambridge Massachusetts. For some time liberals have been denying the superiority of Christianity over other faiths but Ms. Kwok proclaimed the superiority of

Confucianism and Buddhism over Christianity! She also did away with the ideas of sin and guilt. "O Jesus," she said, "who are you that reconciles us to God? Who is this funny God? Who needs to be reconciled with him?" She argued instead for multiple incarnations and reincarnations with Jesus being reincarnated in the endangered environment, specifically as a fig tree. All this from someone who is teaching "Christian" theology to Episcopal seminarians!

While this kind of radical feminism may not be taught in the theological schools of the ACC, be assured that it is coming. The point is that the Episcopal system is almost identical to ours. It is very much an environment where this sort of thing is encouraged and accepted. And this is but one of the directions that current theology is taking. There is no way of knowing what direction it will go in the future as it skitters across the surface of our modern culture. We are in theological free-fall.

(e) Unsound Effects: The Impact of Liberalism

1) On Theological Education

In spite of the lack of common results, mainstream scholars, many of whom teach at our seminaries, remain solidly committed to their basic assumptions. Those who were part of the Jesus Seminar, for example, shared the conviction that the Gospels are "...narratives in which the memory of Jesus is embellished by mythic elements that express the church's faith in him, and by plausible fictions that enhance the telling of the gospel story for first-century listeners who knew about divine men and miracle workers firsthand." (Evans, 1985, p. 3)

These assumptions, or ones much like them, are commonplace in modern biblical scholarship. They are the rules by which the game is played. Even conservative and evangelical scholars (and, contrary to popular belief, there are many of them) who start from the traditional/orthodox understanding of Scripture have to couch their work in terms compatible with these rules. Otherwise they would gain no hearing at all. While there is no doubt that modern scholarship has contributed a great deal to our understanding of Biblical times and customs, its overall impact on the church has been nothing short of devastating.

Basically what has happened is that several generations of prospective Anglican clergy have been plunged into the world of modern scholarship upon their arrival at our theological schools. Their teachers, by and large, have strongly advocated the above-described methodology which is fundamentally at odds with the teaching of the church and unable to provide a commonly acceptable alternative. (How these teachers ever got into and remained in these positions is a complex story beyond the scope of this book.) It is little wonder that many students emerge from theological college not only with less confidence in the classic tenets of the faith than they had before, but also, for some, with a completely different understanding of that faith.

They are especially vulnerable to the pressure they encounter in seminary because their faith had already been under assault in the secular educational system. Now they discover that their teachers of theology share a similar set of assumptions to their counterparts in the university. For many this is a very liberating experience as they discover they can fully accept a modern worldview and at the same time remain in the church.

Their teachers of theology might tell them, for example, that of course one cannot accept the idea that a man could bodily rise from the dead. But that does not mean that you can no longer affirm a belief in the resurrection of Jesus. You can still do this by changing the meaning of the word "resurrection" to refer to the "rise of faith" which the early disciples experienced after the discouragement brought about by the death of Jesus. And so you do. After all, these respected, knowledgeable and authorized teachers of the church have encouraged you to go the way they have gone. In fact, in many cases, theological educators have taken great efforts to attack and destroy the "Sunday School" faith of their students in order to replace it with something more sophisticated and congenial to the modern approach. It has reached the stage in most of our seminaries that it is fair to say that students who continue to hold to the traditional/orthodox positions of the Church do so *despite* their theological education.

This not to say than none of our theological educators, scholars or institutions uphold the faith of the Church. Some do. In fact, Wycliffe College, in Toronto, has made quite a little cottage industry out of being the exception to the rule, attracting many students beyond its natural evangelical Anglican constituency. They come from all over Canada and from various shades of churchmanship in order to get a solid grounding in the Bible. There can be no doubt that its commitment to the centrality of the Scriptures (the school's motto is "Verbum Domini Manet" or "The Word of the Lord Endures") has kept it also as a centre for traditional/orthodox faith in the Canadian Church. It is also worth mentioning that Vancouver's Regent College, a broadly based evangelical theological school with many Anglicans on its staff, is gaining increasing acceptance as a place of training for Anglican ministers.

However, the overall picture drawn in this section remains the normal experience for the majority of our theological students..

2) On the Ordination Process

The irony is that all these students go on to be ordained and promise to uphold the doctrine of the Church, the same doctrine they have found under sustained attack in theological college. Those who have been converted by their professors find their new views to be no barrier to ordination as far as their bishops are concerned. The old requirement to subscribe to the Thirty-Nine Articles has been quietly dropped. Ordination vows are now taken with the shared understanding that the Church is not going to hold candidates to the ordinary and commonly understood meaning of its basic doctrine. A kind of game is being played in which only a few of the spectators know that the rules have all been changed.

This attitude has made a significant contribution to the overall atmosphere within the Church. It has become entirely acceptable, for example, to lead worship with an thoroughly orthodox liturgy while at the same time being in active opposition to what it plainly proclaims. Naturally this has been done at substantial psychological cost and a number of rationalizations have been developed to help deal with the obvious tension. Some justify themselves by saying that they *sing* rather than *say* the Creed, on the grounds that this removes it to the realm of poetry and symbol. From this point of view its normal and literal sense can be transcended, allowing one to make it mean whatever they want it to mean. Others resort to the theory that there is a proper distinction to be made between what one stands for in public, as a representative of the Church, and what one privately believes as an individual.

There is little to recommend such justifications. If all the clergy bought into them it would, in theory at least, be possible to have a situation in which none of the Church's leaders believed in what the Church officially stood for! It is difficult not to see all this as mental gymnastics to avoid the obvious charge of hypocrisy. Could such a thing be tolerated outside the walls of the Church? Imagine, for example, the head of the Boy Scouts admitting that he actually did not like to work with children and that he thought that campfire singing should be banned! The obvious question would be, "Why, then, are you in the Boy Scouts?" Indeed. Perhaps he just likes the uniform.

Given these circumstances, it is little wonder that tremendous pressure was building behind the scenes to do away with the old liturgy and move toward one that is more in line with modern belief. This is one of the main reasons why the BAS was so eagerly received by many bishops and clergy and why it seems so radically different than the BCP. Although the BAS represents a fairly modest shift toward modern theology it really is the first time that such theology has broken surface in the denomination (unless, that is, one counts the "New Curriculum" for Sunday Schools in the 1960's). And, of course, it is also only a way-station on the road to much more radical change as various groups in the church press for liturgies that conform to what they already believe or do not believe anymore.

If anyone finds this account difficult to believe I simply invite him to have some frank conversations with persons who have been ordained in the ACC in the last forty years. Most of those who are close to the system are fully aware that many of our clergy, including bishops, no longer fully accept the traditional/orthodox Christian faith which the Church still officially proclaims. No wonder there is but silence when what used to be heresy is openly proclaimed. After all, who is able to cast the first stone?

Much of this came into dramatic focus for me when a colleague told me of an experience he had as a theological student when doing parish visits as part of his training. The rector had asked him to visit a retired Canadian bishop who had taken up residence in the parish. When my friend arrived he found the elderly gentleman reading his Bible. As he did so he was using his pen to cross out those portions with which he did not agree. While few knowledgeable people would be shocked by such a story nowadays, it is revealing to note that this episode took place in the 1950's! If we make the reasonable assumption that the bishop had come to his convictions during his theological education some forty years before we can see that the kind of behind-the-scenes changes to which I have been referring were already well underway back in the early years of this century. By the 1970's the bubble was about to burst.

3) On Right and Wrong

Liberalism, then, is by its very nature is forever changeable and it has been introduced into an institution which has stood for the same truths for almost two thousand years. This would be destabilizing all by itself but the fact is that many within the Church have continued to espouse the traditional/orthodox position and have no intention of moving away from that commitment or accepting any official departure from it. As long as the official facade of traditional/orthodox Christianity remained and as long as liberals were unwilling or unable to make any changes in official doctrine it was possible to retain some (false) sense of unity.

Liberalism has reached the point of strength, however, at which it is not content to live within the restraints of the official positions of the Church. Having already abandoned adherence to the Bible in matters of doctrine, it is now pushing to do the same in matters of morals and practice and this, by the very nature of things, requires a more public face. After all, it is possible to doubt or reinterpret doctrine, like our retired bishop above, without anyone else necessarily knowing about it. But changes in morality are much more visible, affecting behaviour or lifestyle.

For years liberalism has been content to share the Christian moral consensus which underlaid Western culture. Now, just as the culture has moved away from that consensus so liberalism desires to follow. Deriving its belief systems, not primarily from the Bible, but from some version of secular philosophy, so also it has turned from the morality of the Bible to the "situation ethics" which dominate the thought of the cultural elite. Underlying both these shifts has been the conviction that there is no absolute truth. Liberals are well aware that they themselves hold a bewildering variety of theologies which are all open to change as the culture develops. In this context it is not proper to raise the question of which of these varieties might be the truth. Such a question betrays a lack of understanding of the fundamental rules of the game. According to these, "All truth, is relative". Except, of course, for the truth of that last statement!

It must be said at this point that non-liberals most definitely do not share this conviction. They continue to hold to the now out of fashion idea that when something is said to be true then its opposite must be said to be false. To them, along with vast majority of humanity both past and present, this is self-evident. The idea of the relativity of all truth has only arisen among the cultural elite of European-based cultures. These cultures, now in the process of abandoning the Christian faith upon which they were founded, have been unable to agree on any viable alternative. This, along with a whole complex of other factors, has resulted in giving up on the whole idea of absolute truth. Although this view is beginning to show real signs of disintegration in the culture at large, liberals in the church continue to embrace it. To the liberal mind it is mere arrogance to assert that one has the truth. This is heard again and again in the Church, especially from those in leadership.

A recent example comes from the Primate's address to the last General Synod, when, in reference to Essentials 94, he said that he wanted "...to discourage a tendency to suggest that one group is right and another not- a tendency that moves into issues of power and talk about winners and losers rather than about brothers and sisters." (General Synod 1995 Report, p. 2)

Those who continue to hold to traditional/orthodox Christianity often find such statements non-sensical, intimidating and even self-serving. To them it just doesn't make any sense, for example, to affirm Jesus Christ to be the only Saviour without implying that other views are self-evidently wrong and even possibly un-Christian. Part of their goal is to point this out to their brothers and sisters whom they see as in serious error and in spiritual danger themselves not to mention a threat to the faith of the Church as a whole. It is not so much a question of power as it is a question of truth. At the same time they may hear such statements by those in high positions of authority as direct attempts to silence and disenfranchise them within the denomination. The rules of the game seem to be framed in such a way as to try to keep them off the playing field altogether (see "One Train At a Time, Please" p. 116). Furthermore, the Primate speaks of power as if it is something none of us should seek while he and those who share his views occupy many of the seats of power in the denomination. One can be forgiven, perhaps, if, from this point of view, his comments might be heard as a little bit self-serving.

This is not to imply that the Primate intended his remarks to have these effects. It is much more likely that he was simply unaware that anyone could react in this way. He wants to be open and inclusive but he apparently cannot see that those within the Church who do not share his liberal assumptions actually end up being excluded by them. It is part of the burden of this book to show how this is so and that the inability to recognize this reality lies at the heart of the present crisis in which the Church finds itself. Gone are the days when we fought over such trivialities as whether or not to wear stoles or use candles on the altar. Our division is infinitely deeper, going to the very foundation of what we believe.

(f) Conclusion: Truth or Consequences

We now have within our ranks two different languages, two different ways of thinking and, in fact, two different and incompatible religions. Although this is a drastic conclusion to reach, it is, I believe, the only one which accords with reality. I recognize that some will accuse me of causing division and even schism by saying this. But, in fact, the division is already painfully present. Until both liberals and those in the traditional/orthodox camp recognize this fact they will continue to try to mix oil and water with increasingly frustrating results. Indeed, part of the sense of crisis is the fact that many on both sides are subconsciously aware of this truth but cannot bring themselves to admit it, let alone name it. It is just too monstrous an idea for good Anglicans to consider. It calls into question our history, our identity, our unity and, perhaps most importantly, our future. But that does not make it any less true. We must face the truth and deal with it. There is no other way out of the mess we are in. The truth will set us free.

(ii) What Does It Look Like?: Basic Characteristics of the Liberal Religion

(a) Introduction: Out of Control

Having traced the rise of the liberal religion, it is now necessary to examine some of its specific theological characteristics in order to demonstrate its incompatibility with traditional/orthodox Christianity. In the next chapter I will show how each of the symptoms of the present crisis in the ACC is linked to the introduction of liberalism. The last section of the book will then address the possibilities for recovery.

The nature of liberalism is related to its underlying rejection of the traditional/orthodox view of the nature and authority of the Bible. The failure of the historical-critical method to provide assured results has meant that liberalism has been characterized by variety and changeability. I have no doubt left the impression in many minds that liberals always come to radical conclusions when they study the Bible. This is not so, of course. Many liberals are what we might call moderate critics who propose a picture of Jesus, for example, which is quite similar to that recognized by the traditional/orthodox mind. However, based upon their own assumptions, there is no way for these liberals to demonstrate that they are right and other, more radical critics, are wrong. Once the "control" of the text itself has been abandoned the only "control" left comes entirely from outside the text, from the experience of the particular critic or reader. There is no other source. Therefore, just as the human experience is infinitely variable, so are theologies of liberalism. This leads us directly to a consideration of its first characteristic.

(b) A New Authority Is Given Unto You: The Primacy of Experience

1) Help Wanted: A Guide Through the Ruins

For liberals "experience" has become a primary source of authority. Following a desire for a "scientific" theology, liberals used to imagine themselves to be champions of objectivity. But this is no longer the case. Now it is recognized by liberals themselves that it really is experience which is guiding their reading of the Bible. Instead of recognizing the obvious danger of such unbounded subjectivity, they have made a virtue out of a necessity by accepting experience as an authority superior even to Scripture, reason and tradition! Again and again one encounters statements such as "I know Scripture says that adultery is wrong, but it has been my experience (or, statistics have shown) that in fact adultery can be beneficial to a relationship." This approach has been especially evident in the debate over homosexuality.

It is important to realize that the liberal, at least in his own mind, has not, in making this kind of statement, turned his back on the Bible. However, the Bible from which he draws his inspiration is a vastly different kind of Book than it has been to two millennia of Christians. To him it is a book that reflects the *experience* of Jewish people and early Christians as they encountered the Divine in their lives. It is to be honoured as the source of our particular tradition but it need not be considered more inspired than the Koran or the Book of Mormon. Like all human efforts it full of errors and contradictions. A product of a variety of many religions, cultures and philosophies, its authors portray widely differing views of God and how he relates to humanity. Given this view of the nature of the Bible it makes perfect sense to pick and choose from among its teachings only those which are in accord with our own understanding of the truth. Indeed, we are forced to do this if we expect to make any use of the Bible at all. It has become a smorgasbord from which we can select whatever appeals to us rather than a multi-course dinner carefully prepared and served up by a mother who expects us to eat what is set before us.

If, then, as liberals allege, the Bible is merely the uncertain record of one people's experience of God, then it's authority is reduced dramatically. I say "merely" and "reduced", of course, because this is a big comedown for the Bible from its position in catholic Christianity. There it is considered to be the unique Word of God, inspired by the Holy Spirit, all its parts fitting together into a coherent whole, superior to all other so-called revelations and thus the final authority on faith and practice. For almost two thousand years the church has been sustained and renewed in its doctrine and mission by allowing itself to be shaped again and again by the teaching of the Scriptures. In the Anglican tradition this was, as we have noted, expressed as the Church being "under" the Bible. The fractured and ambivalent Bible of liberalism obviously cannot have such a role. Indeed, in the liberal world the very idea of being "under" any kind of authority is to be challenged. With this view what is needed is a means of picking one's way through the shattered remains of the Biblical tradition. Which bits and pieces of the Biblical tradition are authentic for modern people? Which speak to present reality?

It is clear that in such a system we have to make the necessary choices ourselves. And in this we are guided by our own experience of God within the context of the wider community of our fellow pilgrims. This is assumed to be the work of the Holy Spirit as he/she/it reveals God's direction for the new age. Revelation, then, rather than being confined to the Bible as was previously believed, actually continues in the ongoing life of the church. This "revelation", like that of the Bible, is filled with ambiguity and is not absolute or final. But it is quite capable of calling the teaching of the Bible into question. In this sense the Bible is "under" the church. Thus in order to discern God's word for today one does not primarily look *back* to the Bible but *around* to the experience of the community of God's people and even, ultimately, of one's self. In this system the careful exposition of the Scriptures has been superseded by an attempt to "discern the mind of the Church". Sermons tend to stress what has happened in the life of the preacher, the community, or the world rather than upon the truth of God's written Word. The Sunday School curriculum which focuses on "The Whole People of God" finds a ready market. The model of the preacher in his pulpit and the congregation in their rows of pews is fast being replaced by that of the "facilitator" on his chair within the gathered circle of the encounter group. Here, everyone's experience is a valid experience.

2) Implications For the Church (I)

This new "theology of experience" is commonly accepted and practiced throughout much of the Anglican Church of Canada. In the absence of any common body of beliefs, we have reached the point where if an Anglican holds an opinion then it must be accepted as a valid one. There is no agreed-upon mechanism to help us judge such opinions. For that to become a reality there would have to be clearly articulated and authorized doctrinal standards by which to measure them and, as we have seen, this is precisely what is impossible in today's Church. How then can the Church arbitrate between various opinions and experiences in trying to make up its common mind on particular issues? Asking this question will bring us face to face with one of the more serious implications of having adopted "experience" as the ultimate authority.

The uncomfortable truth is that in such circumstances the only thing that really matters is power, raw political power. That is, it becomes a question of *whose* opinions and experiences will guide the denomination. It cannot be a question of right or wrong for we no longer have any way of answering. Not only that but the liberal mind will not even acknowledge the validity of asking such a question in the first place. All we are left with is power. Who within the denomination has the power to make their opinions count?

This question is complicated by the fact that the authority structure of the ACC suffers from a high degree of ambiguity. In large part this stems from the fact that a hierarchical model (archbishops, bishops, priests, deacons and laity) has been overlaid by a congregational/democratic model (congregations, vestries, diocesan synods and General Synod). The dynamics of the power relationship between these two sources of authority are very complex. They are interconnected in a number of ways. For example, synods elect bishops but synods cannot make decisions without the concurrence of their bishops. However it is probably fair to say that the real power centre of the denomination as a whole lies in General Synod.

Leaving aside the vexing question of who controls General Synod or sets its agenda, the simple truth is that major policy directions of the ACC must gain the approval of this body. It meets every three years and brings together all of the bishops as well as representatives of the clergy and laity from every diocese. In a very rough analogy it can be seen as the Parliament of the Church. As a result General Synod has become the focus and battleground for various interest groups who wish to influence the direction of the denomination. And there is no way to have any idea what direction that will be when you are theological free-fall. No way at all. It only takes a voting majority in General Synod. There is no accepted truth against which its decisions can be measured. There is no effective Constitution or Supreme

Court to which to appeal. The fact that a large majority of "the people of God" might not agree with General Synod is a moot point. They have no vote.

All this is the ultimate result of adopting "experience" as a primary authority in the Church. One can only hope that the "mind of the Church" as expressed in General Synod is indeed the expression of the Holy Spirit. Our tradition, however (as we have seen, p. 11), suggests extreme caution in making such an assumption.

(c) All In the Family: The Need To Be Inclusive

1) Your Experience Is As Good As My Experience

A second basic characteristic of liberalism is its strong emphasis on inclusion. There is little doubt that this attitude arose originally out of a generosity of spirit nurtured within the womb of Anglican comprehensiveness. However, what used to be a way of expressing our diversity within a commitment to a common core of beliefs has now become something quite different. Liberals really seem to want to find a way to include everybody. Every voice is a valid voice. Every opinion is a valid opinion. If you *call* yourself an Anglican Christian then you *are* an Anglican Christian, no matter what theology you might hold. We hear many calls for unity but are never told of what this unity consists other than our common membership in the same Church. By this fact alone we are expected to consider each other's positions just as valid as our own.

It must be recognized that this undefined and hence unlimited inclusiveness is a completely novel idea in the whole history of the church. Not only is it novel but it is completely contrary to both Scripture and tradition. Jesus in fact saved some of his harshest criticism for certain religious professionals of his day who assumed that they, of all people, were part of God's family. Jesus told them they were really children of the devil and the blind leading the blind. He even taught that the church would contain many tares among the wheat and that the former would come under eternal judgment. As far as our tradition is concerned, the Book of Common Prayer calls upon a bishop to "...banish and drive away all erroneous and strange doctrine contrary to God's Word; and both privately and openly to call upon and encourage others to do the same." (p. 663) This is clearly a long way from the spirit of inclusion that has now entered the life of the Church. Some of its proponents have raised it to the level of absolute dogma. Much of the leadership of the Church has adopted it as a fundamental rule by which discussion proceeds. How did this happen? As we have seen it is certainly not part of our tradition or of our official positions.

It happened primarily because inclusivism is a necessary condition to the free exercise of liberalism. The latter is, as we have seen, infinitely variable because it is based on a theological method which no longer has an anchor in the Holy Scriptures (or in any other defined authority). Not only does this result in liberal theologies succeeding one another over time as the culture evolves but also at any one time in the Church there will be a significant number of competing liberal theologies, rooted as they are in the differing experiences of their proponents. To insist that any one of these was to be excluded would raise the problem of the basis for such an exclusion. It would imply that there was a canon or standard of some kind from which the excluded theology had departed.

Liberalism has long since discovered that its methodology is unable to produce such an agreed-upon doctrinal core. It therefore correctly regards any attempt to define such a core as a profound threat. The underlying methodology of liberalism would have to be rejected in the process. Furthermore, if such a core were to be defined it would exclude any number of theologies and their followers who are now bona fide members of the liberal Anglican establishment. Add to this the likelihood that many liberals are well aware of their own personal departure from the official doctrinal positions of the denomination and you can begin to appreciate the attachment to this dogma. Many are naturally very nervous about any possibility of the reimposition of these positions because they themselves would be excluded. For these reasons, among others, liberalism demands inclusivism. It has no choice.

2) Implications For the Church (II)

(A) The Exclusion of Orthodoxy

Before leaving this discussion of inclusivism it is necessary to touch on two serious effects of adopting such a position. The first of these is perhaps more obvious than the second. Here I am referring to the almost self-evident truth that the insistence upon inclusivism has the effect of *excluding* those who still hold to the traditional/orthodox faith which underlies the official doctrines of the Church. These persons continue to insist that there are a number of basic doctrines which everyone in the Church must accept simply because it is difficult to see how anyone could claim to be a Christian while denying them. These doctrines literally define the faith, have always been part of the Anglican way and cannot be surrendered or compromised. Now those who insist upon them are being scolded by many in positions of power who claim that such "exclusivist" views are "intolerant" and "unloving".

Non-liberals, it must be emphasized again, hear these pronouncements as attempts to marginalize and silence them. How can they be expected to feel included in the discussion when some of their basic convictions are excluded from the outset? The insistence upon inclusiveness clearly means that the results of the debate are determined in advance, at least to the extent that the traditional/orthodox position is excluded.

Liberals, if they wish to be truly inclusive should drop this kind of intimidating language and be truly welcoming of all views. After all, as has been pointed out, the traditional/orthodox position is enshrined in the official doctrinal positions of the Church and it seems strange indeed that it is the one that is being frozen out. Strange, perhaps, but logically necessary. The truth is that inclusivists cannot include exclusivists and vice-versa because these concepts are logically incompatible. Inclusivists cannot welcome the conviction that inclusivism is not right. The exclusivist cannot play by the inclusivist's rules. The former has set boundaries and will always be forced by this to make judgments about what views are inside the fence and which are not. He cannot accept all views and he especially cannot accept inclusivism. To do so he would have to exclude himself!

Much of the difficulty in resolving the conflicts in the ACC stem from the inability of either side in the debate to face up to the implications of this reality. Liberals continue to make statements that they think are meant to invite the participation of all Anglicans but which in fact exclude and offend many. On the other hand, traditional/orthodox Anglicans continue to make statements which imply that their own desire for a defined core of "essentials" should be accepted in an institution whose leaders are generally committed to being inclusive. Such statements are instinctively and correctly seen as a threat to the basic belief system of liberals. Naturally they resist and even obstruct. It is only logical. Once again we are at an impasse. There is simply no way forward until both sides accept the fact that we are dealing with two different and incompatible religions. This is the truth that will set us free.

(B) The Threat to Institutional Life

The second implication of "inclusivity" is equally momentous. This is the question of whether or not *any* institution, let alone a church, can long survive with such a principle at its core. As long as this inclusivity remains undefined it will be without limits. Imagine that the Anglican Church as such did not exist but that there were a number of independent congregations across the land, each espousing one of the theologies now within the Church. On what possible basis could they come together? What would make them even want to share the same institution? Any institution needs a reason to exist, a purpose, a mission which all its members share. Above all it needs an identity. Imagine, if you can, the founding convention of a National Church for such congregations. Given the number of strident and diverse voices that would be heard, it is difficult to believe that they could come to any form of agreement about their common identity. It is much easier to believe that those congregations that shared the same theology (be it liberationist, aboriginal, feminist, ecologist, New Age, Marxist or whatever) would band together. This would seem to be a more natural scenario. Could it be that it is only the memory of a former shared identity that is holding the Anglican Church of Canada together?

Coming at it from this perspective suggests a couple of related questions that need to be asked of liberalism. There is little doubt that the crisis in the ACC is related to liberalism being thrown together with traditional/orthodox Christianity. This has led to institutional impasse. *But even if liberalism was on its own would not its commitment to inclusivity and to the primacy of "experience" as an authority form a formidable obstacle to any organizational focus?* There are no examples from history to help us with this question because liberalism has never had to go it alone. It has always started out within a "host" institution and gradually taken it over as much as possible.

Our second question is an outgrowth of the first. *Do we have an example of a liberal institution which was actually formed on the basis of liberal principles?* If we look to the culture around us (from which theological liberalism takes its lead), say to the educational system, we find a similar pattern to the situation in the Church. It too arose when liberal values were as yet unknown and was only subsequently dominated by secular liberalism. Interestingly, it can be argued that even these secular institutions are now in disarray. The dream of inclusivity seems to lead to social chaos.

We are coming to understand that our common life requires a shared set of underlying values in order to survive. It has been my argument that this is absent in the ACC today. Liberalism has done little in the sacred or secular worlds to engender much confidence in its ability to establish and articulate such values. Indeed, secular liberals, such as Todd Gitlin in his recent book, *The Twilight of Common Dreams*, seem to be waking up to this reality. There is a serious message in here for the Church.

(d) To Universalism, and Beyond!

1) Introduction: No Hell

A third basic characteristic of liberalism is universalism. This is the view that all humanity will eventually be "saved". In plain language it simply means that no one is going to go to hell or spend an eternity outside the presence of God. This belief often arises out of the conviction that a loving God cannot, by definition, condemn anyone to everlasting punishment. Besides, such an old-fashioned view puts limits upon God's infinite love for the human race.

2) Contrary To Popular Opinion

This opinion is so pervasive in the ACC that it is a genuine shock to hear anything else. This is in spite of the fact that it clearly contradicts the teaching of Jesus, the whole of the New Testament and the consistent teaching of the Church for two thousand years. There is no Biblical text which, interpreted in context, supports the concept of universalism. On the contrary, it doesn't take much reading of the Bible or of the BCP or of the BAS to see that the whole of our Faith is predicated on the truth that there is a heaven to gain and a hell to shun. Jesus tells us that when he comes in glory at he end of the age he himself, as the King, will be the judge who decides the destiny of every person. The wicked "...will go away to eternal punishment but the righteous to eternal life." (Matt. 25:46) In the passage familiar to all Christians Jesus says:

> For God so loved the world that he gave his one and only Son, that whoever believes in him shall not perish but have eternal life. For God did not send his Son into the world to condemn the world, but to save the world through him. Whoever believes in him is not condemned, but whoever does not believe stands condemned already because he has not believed in the name of God's one and only Son. (John 3:16-18)

When we bring our children for baptism the priest reminds us that "...our Saviour Christ saith, None can enter into the kingdom of God, except he be born anew of Water and the Holy Spirit." (BCP: p. 523) In the funeral liturgy of the BAS we pray "O worthy and eternal Judge, do not let the pains of death turn us away from you at our last hour." (p. 576) Against a background of universalism all this makes little, if any, sense. Rather, the possibility of eternal punishment is part of the warp and woof of our whole liturgical life, from baptism to burial, from Advent to Christ the King. Again and again we pray that we might be granted eternal life based upon the work of Christ. Why would we do this if we are all to be saved anyway?

If the church had not had this perspective from the beginning it could have saved itself an awful lot of theological ink! A person could be driven to despair when contemplating the sheer volume of writing, the intensity of argument, the concentration of energy and the dedication of entire lives that have been wasted. The best minds the church ever produced spent themselves seeking to understand a faith which held to a God of *both* love and judgment. Their deep probings into this paradoxical mystery produced some of the richest veins of contemplation ever explored. Much of the classical Christian understanding of our "free will" and its relationship to the sovereignty of God arises out of this discussion. Driving all of this was a conviction that the Bible was entirely true in its portrayal of God, and that there is great merit for the Christian in accepting and exploring this truth, even and especially when it appears contradictory. God, after all, is beyond all human comprehension.

3) Listening To the Serpent

The reasons that the traditional view has been rejected by liberals are clearly related to their basic theological method. Once you abandon the traditional/orthodox view of Scripture, thus permitting yourself to pick and choose from among the biblical data according to your experience, it is little wonder that the doctrine of eternal punishment is among those first to go. The human heart and mind naturally object to it. Surely, we tell ourselves, as the serpent suggested to Eve, God didn't really say that. Our concept of a loving God precludes such a notion. We have reason enough to set aside this offensive doctrine. Once we no longer have to accept it simply because the Bible so clearly proclaims it, it becomes a definite non-starter.

Simply denying the reality of eternal judgment may seem to enhance the concept of a loving God but in fact it only forces us to deal with the question at another level while at the same time creating other significant problems. For example, if all are eventually saved then presumably human beings are not truly free after all. If no one is able to resist the love of God then human dignity as "free agents" is called into serious question. In a system like liberalism which puts an ultimate value upon freedom and liberation this is a critical consideration. Furthermore, the older defence of human suffering as a result of this freedom is also not available to the universalist. How can a God who will eventually override all resistance to his love continue to stand by in the face of present evil? What reason can be offered for his inaction? Is this truly a God of love?

4) It Just Doesn't Work

These questions suggest that the adoption of universalism has extremely serious implications for the whole of Christian theology. Certainly it could be argued that it turns Jesus into a very unreliable guide to spiritual matters. How can we trust him about eternal life when he is so wrong about eternal death? If he is this unreliable how can we consider him to be the one and only Son of God? Universalism casts doubt on the need for the Cross as the act in which God the Son died for the sins of the world. Perhaps the Cross has some residual power as the ultimate expression of God's love, but this lessens its place in our Faith. Evangelism is no longer a call to repent and be saved but, if anything, an attempt to let people know the "good news" that they are already saved. As a direct result the very essence of the Gospel is altered. The very idea of being saved by faith, or being saved at all, is without foundation.

There can be no doubt that universalism belongs to another belief system altogether than traditional/orthodox Christianity. Just tacking it on does not work. It is like trying to play a CD on your old record player. It just doesn't work. You have to purchase a completely different machine.

To press matters a bit further, universalism is a logical and even necessary extension of the inclusivism that marks liberalism. If being inclusive means that everyone who *claims* to be in the Church *is* in the Church then universalism merely widens the circle to include everyone else. The final frontier has been breached. Once liberalism lost confidence in the possibility of being able to agree on the content of the Gospel it began to realize that it would be logically inconsistent to exclude non-Christians from the kingdom. To do so would imply that such "outsiders" were in mortal error and as we have seen this is simply outside the rules of the game. According to them, again, truth is relative. No one is allowed to say that she is right and thus someone else is wrong. For the same reasons that liberalism leads inevitably to inclusivism it also leads to universalism. It is a slippery slope indeed.

5) Conclusion: Nobody Cares If Everybody Is Saved

It must be said that liberal revisions of the Christian message were all done with the best of intentions. There was a great desire to make the Gospel relevant and more acceptable to modern people. The great irony has been that this revised version of the Gospel has resulted in the Church being more and more marginalized by an uninterested public. How this is related to its inherent universalism was brought home to me in a simple but profound encounter.

I happened to be talking to a very devout Christian who had reluctantly left the Anglican Church for another denomination after many years of faithful service (the kind of conversation, by the way, all too familiar to those of us in local leadership). I asked him for his explanation of the fact that the church was so ineffective in recruiting people to its fold. He had a two-word answer: "Funeral sermons." Startled, I asked for more. "Well," he said, "at my age I go to a lot of funerals and from what I can gather from the sermons everyone goes to heaven no matter what kind of life they lived or what they believed or did not believe. No mention is made of the possibility of judgment or of hell. It is no surprise to me that people don't see any need to go to church. If I believed those preachers I wouldn't either!" At first I wanted to argue with him but he had a point. In fact I have often pondered that conversation. As I have done so, I have been drawn to the conclusion that he is right. Think about it. It has certainly changed my preaching at funerals, one of the few times I have an attentive congregation of the unchurched.

(e) The Legend of the Fall

1) Introduction: I'm OK, You're OK

Underlying all these characteristics of liberalism is a view of human nature which is also contrary to the official teaching of the Church and its Scripture. I refer here to the proposition that human beings are basically good. As such they do not need to be changed so much as to be empowered to be themselves, casting off whatever might offer any restriction. Once again we encounter the central theme of "liberation" found at every level of the liberal program: all the way from using counselling techniques in which individuals "get in touch with their true selves" to advocating social change through revolution as proposed by "liberation theology". This approach incorporates an optimistic view of human nature and denies not only the Fall, but also its corollary, the need for a Saviour. We don't need to be saved, changed or transformed because we ourselves are not sinful. Sin is exterior to us, like a straight-jacket in which we are bound. We need only be freed up to be our true selves. A careful reading of the Eucharistic Prayers in the Book of Alternative Services reveals that they uniformly reflect the view that Jesus came to set us free not from our sin but only from its power over us.

2) God Made Me This Way

This denial of the fall is most evident in so-called "Creation" theology which begins with the affirmation that what God created is good and goes on from there to suggest that what we are deep inside is what God intended us to be (cf. *Original Blessing* [1983] by Matthew Fox). We only need to be set free from the distortions of our true self that has been imposed upon us by tradition or society.

Some liberal theologies are even talking about the divine which is inherent in us all. Getting in touch with it then becomes an essential part of our spirituality. We need not look to the Cross of Christ but within ourselves. In fact, we can, in a sense, save ourselves (even though such language is inappropriate because there is nothing objective to be saved *from* in such schemes).

The effect of this kind of reasoning within the life of the Church is clearly seen in the debate over homosexuality. Many now conclude that because homosexuals are "born this way" then they are simply part of God's good creation. End of argument.

3) Taking the Fall

The Scripture, on the other hand, is abundantly clear that although God did pronounce the Creation "good" upon its completion, sin was subsequently introduced into the world through the disobedience of Adam and Eve. This changed everything. Evil and wickedness entered our very soul. Jesus, in an breathtakingly casual manner, referred to his listeners as "evil" and taught that sinful deeds arose out of sinful hearts (Matt. 7:11, 15:19). According to St. Paul all of those descended from Adam are "in Adam" and are subject to sin and death (Rom. 5:12). All of us are sinful by nature and, in fact, all have actually committed sinful acts as well.

The whole structure of our salvation is erected upon this foundation. We need a Saviour. "While we were yet sinners", Paul tells us, "Christ died for us." (Rom. 5:8) We need some way to have our sin removed and to be placed "in Christ". Unable to do this ourselves we recognize that it can only be done by an act of the grace of God. This traditional/orthodox understanding is powerfully expressed in the Exhortation at the beginning of the Baptism service in the BCP:

> Dearly beloved in Christ, seeing that God willeth all men to be saved from the fault and corruption of the nature which they inherit, as well as from the actual sins which they commit, and that our Saviour Christ saith, None can enter into the kingdom of God, except he be born anew of Water and of the Holy Spirit, I beseech you to call upon God the Father, through our Lord Jesus Christ, that he will grant to this Child that which by nature he cannot have: that he may be baptized with Water and the Holy Spirit, and received into Christ's holy Church, and be made a living member of the same. (p. 523)

4) Conclusion: It Still Doesn't Work

All of the above elements of Christian faith are either explicitly rejected by liberals or implicitly contradicted by the logic of liberalism. It makes little sense to say these words while at the same time hold to universalism and the basic goodness of the human person. Again we have come up against the familiar reality that liberalism and the traditional/orthodox theology of our official doctrinal standard are fundamentally incompatible, representing as they do, two different religions.

(f) Reality Check: Bishop Ingham Speaks Out

Some of my readers may feel that I have been dealing too much in generalities and in theory. There is some justification for this view. I have striven mightily (with some success, I might add) to avoid getting into personalities, finger-pointing, or "he said"-"she said" scenarios. Such approaches are ultimately unproductive and need to be avoided. At the same time, I am not merely shadow-boxing with the bogeyman of liberalism! Real people live by these ideas. I have stated on several occasions that many of them are in positions of authority in the Anglican Church of Canada. It would be irresponsible not to provide at least one specific example of what I mean in order to put some flesh on my arguments and assure my readers that I have at least one foot in contact with the ground.

As it turns out, one of our most prominent bishops, Michael Ingham of New Westminster (Vancouver), has recently provided an excellent case in point. In an address entitled "To Whom to Bow", the bishop deals with precisely the issues I have raised in the above argument. The full text is available in the Summer 1997 edition of "INCOURAGE" (see Appendix A for address). It is a clear and straightforward presentation of liberalism at work and is recommended reading for all Anglicans. We should all be grateful for Ingham's willingness, as a bishop, to speak out so clearly and forcefully.

In his article Ingham defines "inclusivism" as the conviction that while salvation is possible for non-Christians it is still somehow through Jesus Christ alone. That is, if a Muslim finds himself in heaven it is because of the work of Christ even though he did not know anything about it. All that is required is that he "hold sincerely to the path and desire of genuine knowledge of God in whatever way is open to him".(p. 8) If he does so, the salvation won by Christ is extended to him. He becomes a sort of honourary Christian. In this view Christianity remains the ultimate faith but its borders are extended to include all sincere believers of other faiths.

The "pluralist" position, which the bishop holds, goes rather further than this. It refuses to put Christianity above any other religion. All the "great religions of the world offer authentic pathways to God" (p. 8) in and of themselves. They have no need of Christ or his salvation. Rather, all these religions have a way in which the individual can know the fullness of God. Seeing Jesus as divine is the Christian expression of this common theme. Other ways in other traditions are equally valid for their adherents. Christianity has nothing to offer that they don't already have. It may have something to offer those of no particular religion or "whose lives are set on a destructive path" (p. 9) but the bishop is vague as to who these people are and what the church can do for them beyond committing itself to peace and justice.

What Bishop Ingham really objects to is what he calls "Christian Exclusivism". This is the traditional/orthodox view that Jesus Christ is the only Saviour and that the church is under orders to present him as such to non-Christians. Ingham quotes a "speaker" at Essentials 94 (actually it is the world-renowned scholar and author J.I. Packer) to this effect: "We are obligated in practice to evangelize on the basis there is no salvation for anyone whom you encounter apart from faith in Christ." The bishop then refers to

The Montreal Declaration of Anglican Essentials which declares Jesus to be "...the only Saviour; penitent faith in him is the only way of salvation" (from Article 4). Ingham then comments:

> The basic problem with [Christian exclusivism] in my view is not so much its inherent bigotry, which is astonishing to anyone who has close friends among people with other faith traditions, or who has any exposure to the spiritual depth of other great world religions; the basic problem is its implicit doctrine of God...a God that is repugnant and abhorrent. That God should actually condemn everyone who is not joined to the church ...defies all moral sense and contradicts everything we know about God from the witness of Scripture and from the life of Jesus himself. (p. 7)

Some of my more conservative readers may feel like crying in frustration after reading this last sentence. *You know perfectly well that it is the clear and straightforward "witness of Scripture" and of Jesus that the Bishop is rejecting.* How can he make such a statement? It seems to be blindly stupid or even perverse. It is neither. What must keep in mind is that the liberal Bible is a smorgasbord from which you can legitimately reject some parts and accept others. Or perhaps it is better pictured as pot of stew from which each diner can select or reject various ingredients according to preference. In this fashion each could in some sense claim to have eaten the "stew" even though they may have had only the carrots. Thus any particular combination of *accepted* parts of the Bible can be called "the witness of Scripture". Those texts that contradict this witness are simply eliminated from consideration. Either they are directly removed by modern biblical criticism as inauthentic or they are radically re-interpreted. If you can throw out the onions and change the turnip into carrots, you then can enthusiastically eat the altered stew which remains.

This is exactly the process used by Bishop Ingham when asked how he can reconcile his position with what Jesus says in John 14:6: "I am the way, the truth and the life. No one comes to the Father except through me." Now anybody just reading that statement would have to say that it is a pretty exclusivist saying (not to say arrogant or even bigoted!). Ingham's first line of defense is to cast doubt on the "authenticity" of this quotation. "The issue here" he says, "is whether Jesus said those words at all." (p. 9) He goes on to present a scholarly theory which holds that these words were put into Jesus' mouth around the end of the first century by a "Johannine" Christian community. Under Jewish oppression their attitudes began to harden and they created a version of Jesus that is more compatible with their new absolutist views. Thus the sayings of Jesus in the Gospel of John are especially suspect. As Bishop Ingham puts it, "The question is do they arise from the Johannine community or are they found on the lips of Jesus?" (p. 9) In other words, the

Jesus of history did not really say these words and therefore they can be safely ignored.

But even if we insist on going against this scholarly opinion and accept the saying as authentic, there is a second line of defense. Here it is best to quote the Bishop more or less in full.

> Then the question arises: 'What do they mean? ...to whom are the words addressed?' Remember that these words are spoken in context of conversation with Thomas ...who says 'Lord we do not know the way, show us the way.' And Jesus says 'I am the way'. It could well be that Jesus is saying that 'no one of *you* comes to the father but by me'. But the church in its later years interpreted that as an absolute statement covering every human being on the face of the earth. Other ways of interpreting this statement could be this: if I were to say to you what is the way to Vancouver from Victoria: Well it's that way...its North and East. Is there one path to get there? No there are several paths from here to Vancouver, but there is one way. So it is possible, and the inclusivists would argue this, that Christ is present on every path because he is the Way. And I think that is quite a supportable interpretation. (p. 9)

Putting aside the question of whether or not such an interpretation is at all credible, for us it is only important to note that it has the effect of turning a clearly exclusivist saying of Jesus into an inclusivist one. The obvious straightforward meaning of the text has been reversed, turned inside out. This, my friends, is the liberal Bible. It is putty in your hands. You can make it say whatever you want it to say.

The question then becomes "What do you want it to say?". In the case before us Bishop Ingham wants it to say that sincere followers of world religions are included in God's salvation. Their way to heaven is just as valid as the Christian way. A straightforward reading of Scripture does not yield this doctrine. If it did all Christians would long ago have come to this position. But they did not. As the quotation below demonstrates, Bishop Ingham is fully conscious of the fact that the Church has consistently proclaimed the opposite to be true for two millennia. That he pronounces such terrible judgment upon his own heritage raises many questions that go far beyond the scope of this book to address. What remains important for our discussion is to discover upon what basis he can so confidently set aside the great weight of biblical material which led the church to its exclusivist doctrine. What is it that has more authority than the very words of Scripture?

It is clearly what I have called "experience". As I have pointed out earlier in this chapter, liberals have replaced the authority of Scripture with the authority of experience. In Bishop Ingham's case he makes this quite clear himself. He tells us that he has personally had the privilege of having close friends who belong to other world religions and they are perfectly fine people who exhibit no need of salvation. He has also been exposed to the spiritual depth of their various faiths.

> We have historically believed our religion to be superior to everyone else's. It is only in the modern world that we have come to regard with shame some of our own history. As we have come to live as modern people in Canada, side by side with people of other faith traditions, and have come to know them as colleagues and friends, it is only in recent times that this belief in Christian absolutism has been questioned by Christians themselves. (p. 7)

Having had these experiences he feels free to characterize other Christians, who still hold to the traditional position of the Church, as bigots. While such language is indeed unfortunate it clearly reveals the depth of his conviction. What he has learned from "experience" is superior to what he has learned from the Bible. Once having accepted this new doctrine he tries to make the Bible agree. It turns out that he has brought his own can of peas and slipped them into the stew so that he can pick them out and enjoy them later. Unless, of course, they turn to mush.

(g) Facing the Facts: Liberalism is Not Just Any Old Religion

Enough has now been said to support my contention that liberalism and traditional/orthodox Christianity are in fact two different and incompatible religions. They are in conflict at every level, from basic assumptions to liturgical formulations. I recognize that it is a very serious matter to make such a claim. Therefore some further elucidation is in order.

Certainly from the point of view of liberals, the notion that they worship a different God must be at best puzzling and at worst inconceivable or offensive. But, from the point of view of traditional/orthodox Anglicans it is a valid and even necessary conclusion. It is extremely important for liberal Anglicans to understand this if they truly desire to listen to every voice in the Church. I certainly have no wish to offend anyone, least of all fellow Anglicans, but I am compelled to say this and to say it as clearly as I can because from where I sit it is simply the truth.

Traditional/orthodox Anglicans, consistent with their assumptions, have no option but to see liberalism as a different religion. Liberalism, equally consistently, denies even the possibility of any such distinction. It is clear that the real problem is rooted in the differing assumptions that each side brings to the debate. This is at least part of the reason that we find it so difficult to talk to one another, to really listen to each other's voice. We recognize, even subconsciously, that our very right to exist is called into question by the position of our fellow Anglicans. No wonder we call each other "bigots" or "heretics"! This is harsh language but it is nevertheless true language. It exposes our fundamental division, a division that goes to the very heart of things, to the very purpose and mission of the church.

It makes little sense for liberals to talk about worshipping a different God or having a different religion. As I have pointed out, it is a fundamental liberal principle that all religions are, in fact, worshipping the same God even though they may well have different understandings of who he/she/it might be like. Religions are merely the codification and symbolic expression of a people's experience of God and no one of them can be said to be the only authentic one. Thus Judaism is the result of the religious experience of Israel, Christianity that of the followers of Jesus, Shamanism that of aboriginal Canadians, Hinduism that of parts of India, etc. These are all human attempts to grapple with the divine which is itself fundamentally beyond human thought and language.

Therefore from the perspective of right and wrong it would seem that it is not an ultimately serious matter for a liberal to be charged with being a follower of a different religion than traditional/orthodox Christianity. For her this does not imply any departure or apostasy at all. It is only a way of saying that different symbols are being used to represent the continuing (and necessarily unfolding, changing) understanding and experience of God in the community. To vision God differently, to attribute different characteristics to him/her/it, than someone else does is necessary and healthy. So if your God is a male monarch (i.e., a king) and mine is a pregnant female we are dealing with the same reality in different clothes. Both expressions are authentic and valid if they genuinely arise out of the experience of those that employ such symbols. That is the criterion. Within such a framework it is literally nonsensical to raise the possibility of worshipping other gods. There are no other gods. There are just different understandings and symbols of the same divine reality.

The only problem with this whole approach to religion, as we have seen, is that it stands opposed to the consistent witness of Holy Scripture and the teaching of the Church for 2000 years!

> And God spoke all these words:
> I am the LORD your God, who brought you out of Egypt,
> out of the land of slavery.
> You shall have no other gods before me....
> You shall not misuse the name of the LORD your God,
> for the LORD will not hold anyone guiltless who misuses his name. (Exodus 20: 1-3 & 7)

> Therefore God exalted him to the highest place
> and gave him the name that is above every name,
> that at the name of Jesus every knee should bow,

> in heaven and on earth and under the earth,
> and every tongue confess that Jesus Christ is Lord,
> to the glory of God the Father. (Philippians 2: 9-11)

> Almighty God, who by thy blessed Apostle has taught us that there is none other name given among men whereby we must be saved, but only the Name of our Lord Jesus Christ: Grant we beseech thee, that we may ever glory in this Name, and strive to make thy salvation known unto all mankind; through the same Jesus Christ our Lord, who liveth and reigneth with thee and the Holy Spirit, one God, for ever and ever. Amen. (BCP, p. 320)

Between these two religions there can be no compromise. As our Lord pointed out:

> *No one sews a patch of unshrunk cloth on an old garment, for the patch will pull away from the garment making the tear worse. Neither do men pour new wine into old wineskins. If they do, the skins will burst, the wine will run out, and the wineskins will be ruined.* (Matthew 9: 16-17a)

(h) Conclusion: Even Coyotes Can't Fly

There is one more point which still needs to be made. I recognize that for the sake of clarity I have been forced to make abstractions from reality. This means that I have often had to make hard and fast distinctions in a world which does not lend itself readily to such analysis. There is no way to avoid this process but it does have its dangers.

One of these, for me, has been that I may have left the impression that the Anglican Church of Canada is made of up of two distinct camps: traditional/orthodox Christians on the one hand and liberals on the other. Such, of course, is not the case. Most of us are somewhere on a spectrum between these options, partly because we are confused and partly because we have not disciplined ourselves to consider the implications of some of the positions we adopt.

I recall a member of the clergy confessing to me that she could accept all the traditional doctrine of the Church with the exception of the Virgin Birth. This did not make her a non-Christian or call into question her salvation. But it did put her whole belief-system at serious risk. In this one area she had decided to put aside the teaching of Scripture. She gave no reason why she drew the line there and not at the bodily resurrection of our Lord (other than her own opinion on the "evidence"). If she were to apply consistently the same principles to the rest of the Bible, as many others have, she would undoubtedly change many of her convictions and fall more completely into the liberal camp. She could certainly not object to others coming to more radical conclusions than her own. Its just a matter of opinion.

The same situation applies to the creeping universalism one finds extant in the Anglican Church. Many have enthusiastically embraced this theory without pausing to consider what it actually entails. They have no intention of changing their understanding of Jesus or of the Cross or of the mission of the Church. But, as I have tried to explain above, all of these doctrines and more are modified or even made redundant by a belief in universalism. Even though an individual can become a universalist and remain traditional/orthodox in the rest of his faith he is merely being inconsistent, a human failing we all share. Even me.

We might call this the "Wile E. Coyote" principle. Most of us who grew up with television will recognize this aspect of serious theological reasoning. It comes from the "Roadrunner" cartoons, nearly all of which had Wile E. Coyote trying some harebrained scheme to catch the ever-elusive Roadrunner (Beep! Beep!). Usually, however, Wile E. is tricked by the speedy bird and finds himself going off the edge of the canyon. There he remains suspended for a moment or two until the realization dawns on him that he is in serious trouble. Then gravity takes over. Down he goes, disappearing into a tiny dot down below! There is a satisfying THUD! when he finally hits bottom.

So it is with traditional/orthodox Christians who adopt any of the principles of liberalism. For a while the rest of their belief system will remain intact. Eventually, however, gravity will take over. It always does. The difference between their fate and that of Wile E. is only this: for them there is no bottom to the canyon. They have fallen into the abyss.

CHAPTER FOUR

It's Liberalism, Eh!

For the time will come when men will not put up with sound doctrine. Instead, to suit their own desires, they will gather around them a great number of teachers to say what their itching ears want to hear. They will turn away from the truth and turn aside to myths. (2 Timothy 4: 3-4)

(i) Introduction: Liberalism is the Problem

The last chapter explored the nature of liberalism, demonstrating that it is different from and opposed to the traditional/orthodox Christianity upon which the ACC was founded. The resulting confusion and confrontation lies at the heart of the malaise which afflicts the denomination. Indeed, it has led to a kind of stalemate as the two religions pull in opposite directions. This is bad enough, of course, but the problem is much deeper than a mere standoff between competing factions in the Church. This chapter will revisit the various symptoms of the crisis that were examined in Chapter Two in order to show that liberalism in and of itself constitutes a serious problem. It has had a generally negative effect on the life and witness of the Church. *The truth is that many of the aspects of the present crisis in the Church either find their origin in liberalism or have been made much worse by its influence.*

It must be emphasized from the start, however, that I do not mean to imply that liberalism is the sole cause of our troubles. Just the major one. Some of our decline, for example, must be laid at the feet of our unwillingness to reach out beyond the middle class, our stubborn refusal to adapt our worship to contemporary realities and our pre-occupation with the proper form of liturgy while at the same time neglecting its true purpose as a vehicle for the heartfelt worship of Almighty God. While these matters, and others, are serious indeed, they must remain secondary considerations when placed in the shadow of liberalism. In fact, we are being so shaken by the enormity of the present crisis that we will no longer be able to hold on so tenaciously to these all too typically Anglican attitudes. In this sense there is a silver lining in the clouds that surround us. But now it is necessary to fly into the eye of the storm itself.

(ii) Returning to the Scene of the Crisis

(a) SYMPTOM 1: The Membership Blues (Reprise)

In Chapter Two I merely presented the bare fact that the ACC has experienced a precipitous drop in membership over the last thirty-five years. The loss of so many members has not been a pleasant or healthy experience for the Church. It has most emphatically not been a case of losing the deadweight or of returning to our "natural" levels after a period of extraordinary growth. It has been a real loss and, it is now important to realize, it has a real connection with liberalism. In order to understand this connection it is necessary to probe deeper into the various ways in which Anglicans have slipped away.

1) The Departed

Like every human organization, denominations experience a loss of fringe members as a part its natural life. One of the saddest realities of parish life in the ACC, however, has been the steady exodus of some of our most involved and committed lay people. It parallels the infamous "brain drain" of our best and brightest Canadians down to the United States. Why are they leaving? This is the critical question but it is one that the official Church has chosen to not to ask. It has many resources which could have been used in order to ascertain precisely what the problems are but this has not been done. In the unfortunate absence of a more scientific investigation it is necessary to fall back on what is the common experience of many parish priests. When someone is leaving the Church they will often seek to explain their actions to their pastor. This is a valuable if painful source of information. Another is conversations with the seemingly endless supply of former Anglicans who now belong to other denominations. All too many begin with "Oh, I grew up in the Anglican Church..." or "We used to go to St. John's...".

Many of these people make it clear that they are not leaving because they want to but because they feel they must. They claim to have discerned trends in our Church, especially at the National level, which they consider to be contrary to the Word of God. They have been disappointed with the inability or unwillingness of the leadership to proclaim clearly the Gospel in its traditional/orthodox shape. They have also come to the conclusion that there really is no hope for change, no possibility that recent trends can be halted, let alone reversed. With much anguish of soul for themselves and great stress to their parishes they have quietly departed taking their energy, talents and money with them.

One of the greatest frustrations for those in local leadership is to see this happening and not be able to do anything about it. We agree with them that here are serious problems in our Church and we too feel powerless to effect change. However, for various reasons we have not come to the conclusion that leaving is the best solution. For us the frustration at seeing them leave is much worse because our hopes for renewal and reformation diminish as fewer and fewer sympathetic people are left behind to carry on the struggle from within. On the other hand it seems true that those of more liberal persuasion are not unhappy to see these kinds of parishioner depart because they did not cooperate in the implementation of the liberal agenda.

Former Anglicans thus continue to help populate the pews of those denominations that have remained unequivocally committed to the essentials of traditional/orthodox Christianity. Many of them express deep regret, missing especially beauty of the liturgy and the life of the sacraments. Such sentiments, however, are not enough to make them change their minds. The slow march continues.

Jesus said that the sheep know the voice of the shepherd. The sheep "...follow him because they know his voice. But they will not follow a stranger: in fact, they will run away from him because they do not recognize a stranger's voice." (John 10:4-5) Is this the spiritual reality that lies behind the exodus of thousands of once-faithful Anglicans? Is the voice of liberalism a "stranger's" voice? Is this why so many have "run away"? This is the essence of the challenge presented to the Church by this type of "leaver".

2) The Nearly Departed

It needs to be said at this point that there is yet another class of dropouts. These are people who have become so discouraged about the state of the ACC at all levels that they have simply become inactive while not actually leaving. A lot of these persons were traumatized by the way in which the BAS was introduced into many parishes. Rightly or wrongly they feel that they were robbed of their way of worship, which for an Anglican is a mortal wound. They have no comprehension of the reasons why the BAS was so eagerly received and the BCP so effectively sidelined. Some of them even felt obligated to leave their home parishes and become wandering gypsies camping in another parish for a while until the BAS takes over there, necessitating another disencampment. It is a trail of tears. Others, less determined or more discouraged, have kept up their membership in their local parish but almost never attend. To the extent that liberalism was behind not only the BAS but the way in which it was so eagerly introduced (even imposed), it must shoulder a major share of responsibility for these less visible "dropouts".

3) Smothering Sunday

While we are considering these questions it might be worthwhile to ask ourselves "Where have all the young men gone?" In a Church that is greying one expects a predominance of females. But something else seems to be at work as well. For not only are older men absent but also there are relatively few younger men. In this area the ACC shares in the overall failure of the Christian church in our culture to attract males. But the suspicion remains that they are *especially* absent from our Church. This is especially odd in an institution which has supposedly been molded by an exclusively male hierarchy. On the surface one would expect such an institution to attract men with ease. This is not the case.

One reason for the relative absence of younger men may be what might be called the feminization of the church, a process that took place long before women were accepted into the ranks of the ordained. It is commonplace knowledge that women have, in recent years at least, formed the backbone of the "workers" within the ACC. For whatever reasons they are the ones who have rolled up their sleeves and done a great deal of the necessary work. Sometimes this was done through the Anglican Church Women (often the saviour of many a parish budget) or through the official and unofficial offices open to them as lay persons in the church. They have taught in the Sunday School, visited the sick, run the bazaars, served on vestries, become layreaders, chaired and staffed committees, gone to synods, done stints as wardens etc. Many a rector has found that the *real* power in a parish was vested in the local matriarch! Without the enormous contribution of these women the ACC would have had to fold up its tents long ago. But you won't find much reference to them in the history books.

Why has this happened? If you listen to the women themselves one often hears the lament that they had to do this work because their men-folk refused. It is possible to argue that it is hardly any wonder such a female-dominated church (at least in the actual activities of lay people) would not be very appealing to most men. They don't tend to show up at Tupperware parties either! But surely this begs the question. At some point, perhaps even within living memory, it is clear that the ACC became relatively unattractive to males in our culture. Naturally this is a troubling development for an institution which is in such need of revitalization. It is a well-known fact among professional observers that if father goes to church it is likely that his wife and family will too. Not only is this true, but there is a much greater probability that his children will also continue to be part of the church when they grow up. If it is only mother who goes to church, the reverse is true. Therefore any Church which appeals so predominately to the female gender will probably continue to decline. It will also find itself suffering further from fragmentization as modern families struggle for wholeness.

What has been the role of liberalism is this area? Without denying that there is a variety of reasons for the "feminization" of the church in general, the ACC has been particularly hard hit because of its current style of pastoral ministry. Even though the male sex was in control of the hierarchy, the denomination came to see the Christian faith in largely feminine categories. The fact that this development arose simultaneously with liberalism is, I would argue, no coincidence. In fact, with the loss of any need, desire or ability to evangelize (see especially "Of Decayed Evangelism", p. 93ff.), much more of the work of the Church became focussed upon its own membership. Today the clergy are largely chaplains to those who attend.

Almost the entire emphasis in such ministry is put on pastoral care, the looking after one's own instead of winning the world for Christ. We became an exclusively nurturing, caring, empathetic, accepting, loving, listening, non-judgmental, and affirming community. While there is much to be said in favour of most of these things, other more male-oriented aspects of the faith were downplayed. Any suggestion of aggression, even protective or progressive aggression (as in the use of military metaphors or in evangelism) became verboten. Anything that reeked of strength or dominance or victory was shunned. In this context, the introduction of female priests was perfectly logical development. That God is being addressed by many in feminine similes and metaphors, with some even calling for goddess worship also comes as no surprise.

In the light of all this it seems reasonable to suggest that men became more and more alienated from an increasingly feminized church. Where could their maleness find expression and acceptance? Where was there room for decisive bold leadership or for an all-out commitment to a great cause? Instead of being enrolled (male and female!) as soldiers in the battle against "the world, the flesh and the devil" (BCP) at baptism, now prayers are made that new Christians be given "an inquiring and discerning heart, a courage to will and to persevere, a spirit to know and love [the Lord] and the gift of joy and wonder in all [his] works" (BAS). While the liturgy was in the process of being "softened", even feminists like the satirist Nancy White, were discovering that "Daughters of Feminists" still wanted to play with Barbies. In spite of all the propaganda that would suggest otherwise, boys will be boys and girls will be girls. When a Church fails to provide adequate psychic space for half of the human race it can expect to be only half full. The ancient metaphor of Mother Church has taken on a whole new reality. For most men it is not an attractive reality.

Liberalism also effectively serves to cut off the Church from those movements which are proving effective in encouraging men to be active in the church. Canadian Anglicanism seems almost untouched, for example, by the Promise Keepers. Many liberals (incorrectly) see its clear call for men to take their rightful and biblical role as leaders in the home and in the church as a call for a return to male domination. Jumping to this conclusion may cause them to miss an opportunity to offer men a place to stand. Promise Keepers also, like most of these organizations, has a Statement of Faith which commits it to the traditional/orthodox Christian faith. This, too, makes it anathema to liberals. Thus it seems that the ACC can only stand and watch as other Churches see more of their men return to the pews.

4) Services No Longer Required

While the categories of "leavers" already discussed can no doubt account for much of the membership decline in the ACC, there remains one more that may be more numerous than all the others put together. These are those for whom the Church has simply become irrelevant. Again it must be acknowledged that this fate is not unique to the Anglican Church. For a variety of reasons Canadian society has turned its back on institutional religion as a whole. What needs not to be overlooked however, is the fact that those denominations which have continued to affirm clearly their commitment to the essentials of traditional/orthodox Christianity have in large part not been plagued by massive defections. They have held their own or even grown some. Some newer denominations, such as the Pentecostals, have indeed thrived.

There are no doubt many reasons why this is true. I would like to suggest a few which, in the context of this book, seem to me to be the most important. First of all, by its very nature, liberalism cannot present a unified or easily understood message to those uninitiated into its mysteries. It constantly is "morphing" into a different shape as new theories take hold in scholarly circles. Traditional language and symbols are retained while at the same time their meaning is in constant flux. Trying to decipher what is really being said is like trying to guess where the pea is in a kind of theological shell game. Will the real Jesus please stand up! As a result liberalism is much better at telling us what it rejects than what it affirms. It is caught in a web of confusion due to it's tendency to be in constant change and it's inability to use straightforward language in explaining itself. For these reasons at least, it finds it extremely difficult to win or retain the allegiance of many ordinary people.

However there is a deeper problem. As we saw in the previous chapter, at the heart of liberalism are its basic principles of the ultimate authority of experience, of universalism and of inclusivism. For most people this boils down to one simple "truth": in the long run it does not really matter what one believes. Whether you are a Christian or a Muslim or an atheist we are headed for the same destination. The God who is love will embrace us all. Where is the incentive here to go to a meeting every week and give up a good percentage of my income to boot? With so many other demands upon a person's time and energy and without the encouragement of a society in which going to church is the thing to do, it is little wonder that so many have walked away from the Church. Who can blame them?

This brings us to a final irony. Liberalism began as an attempt to "adjust" the teaching and practice of the church to fit in with modern thinking. This was done in order to save the church from itself, from continuing to present a hopelessly outdated message to a culture committed to the new ideas of science and technology. As a number of observers have noted, however, as the "faith" was reshaped in order to be acceptable to current thinking, it began to look more and more like that thinking itself. This is hardly surprising because in adopting secularist assumptions liberalism had already committed itself to a secularized version of Christianity. Many people began to notice that the message of the liberal church was largely a baptized echo of certain strains within secular society coming exclusively from the cultural and academic elite. Even if one agreed with this message, it was easily seen that church membership might be redundant. Why go to Church when basically the same message was being proclaimed elsewhere? On the other hand, to the extent that they were opposed to the musings of the cultural and academic elite they would find Church irritating at best and offensive at worst. Why go to church under these conditions? Why indeed?

5) Liberalism's Silent Partner

And so we come to consider what is perhaps the only really hard fact that we have in this whole discussion: *whenever liberalism has become dominant in a denomination (e.g.: the so-called "mainline" denominations) there is always serious numerical decline*. This is a universal truth across cultures, languages and nationalities. It is an observable fact, chronicled by many. One of the most recent authors to do so in detail is Thomas C. Reeves in his 1996 book *The Empty Church: The Suicide of Liberal Christianity.* The opposite also holds true: whenever liberalism has not gained a serious foothold in a denomination (e.g.: the "evangelical" denominations and in Eastern Orthodoxy) such numerical decline has not taken place. Canadian Anglicans need to be aware that the Anglican Church in the Third World, such as Africa and South America, is experiencing significant growth. It is no coincidence that they are largely untouched by liberalism. The conclusion, then, is as obvious as it is irrefutable. Liberalism is a major cause of membership loss. It is that simple.

6) Conclusion: A "Culture of Leaving"

And so they have left. They have left with many others and for many reasons. It must be appreciated that all these leavings have not left unaffected those parishioner who do remain active. Most of our parishes are quite small and when key people leave or drop out the burden falls on fewer and fewer shoulders. Besides, those who have left are people they know and love. They are friends and often even family. When one suffers we all suffer. Naturally this has had a profound negative affect on general morale. Much more serious in some parts of the Church than in others, it is impossible to gauge the way in which this kind of subterranean disaffection might impact upon any movement towards reform.

There is thus what might be called a "culture of leaving" within the Anglican Church. This is different from what some have called the "circulation of the saints" which some other denominations experience. The latter have people coming and going all the time and some of their growth is attributable to the patterns of this movement among the already converted. Unfortunately Anglicans have generally known this to be a one-way street. People leave by the back door all right, but they are failing to come in the front door at anywhere near the same pace. This is demoralizing for the ones who remain. But if they are still looking for the major reason why all of this has happened to their beloved Church, the short answer is: "Its liberalism, eh!".

(b) SYMPTOM 2: Of Decayed Evangelism (Reprise)

The discussion of this topic in Chapter Two ("The Reality of Evangelism", p. 18) ended by noting that the Anglican Church of Canada, just when it needed to evangelize in order even to survive, seemed unwilling or unable to move much beyond talking about this aspect of the faith. What follows will demonstrate that the major reason for this dilemma is the heavy influence of liberalism within the denomination. This can be seen most clearly through a discussion of evangelism in the context of the mission of the Church.

1) Plan "A": One Christ Fits All

Since its inception and until very recently, the church has seen its overall mission in terms of bringing the whole of creation (at least in principle) into the kingdom of God. This was in obedience to Christ's great commission to"go and make disciples of all nations, baptizing them in the name of the Father and of the Son and of the Holy Spirit, and teaching them to obey everything I have commanded you." (Matt.28:19-20) This is an unambiguous command to bring all persons to Christ out of all the peoples, races, cultures and religions of the world. This in turn is based on the clear biblical teaching that any person who is not a believer in Jesus Christ is "condemned already" (John 3:18) and needs to be converted in order to enter the kingdom of God. Eternal life will be granted only to those who repent and put their trust in Jesus Christ alone. Jesus himself made this astonishing claim: "I am the way and the truth and the life. No one comes to the Father except through me." (John 14:6)

And so we find the early church busily engaged in this project from the beginning, first among the Jews and then among the pagans of the day. It recognized that to come to Christ meant to reject any other way of salvation. Ever since, the church has taken this as a given even if, for various reasons, it did not always act as if it did.

England was one of the pagan countries evangelized and eventually converted to Christianity. This is an essential part of our history, sharing as we do in the developments since that time within the Church of England. Indeed the history of Canada itself was shaped by this impulse as first French Catholic missionaries accompanied the earliest European explorers and then the English arrived along with their missionaries from the Church of England. This became part of the great missionary movement of the nineteenth century. While it is true that there was much left to be desired in the ways in which this enterprise was carried out, it was all done in response to Christ's unambiguous command.

2) Plan "B": Different Christs for Different People

While all of this was taking place on the ground, liberalism was gaining adherents among the leadership of the church and this has led to radical change on the mission front. The problem is that the basic principles of liberalism are in serious conflict with the evangelistic emphasis of traditional mission activity. These principles arise out of a new approach to Scripture which has led to a multiplicity of views as to who Jesus is and what it means to follow him. From this perspective the Church does not have a single Christ to present to the non-Christian. To whom are they to convert? This core of uncertainty at the heart of liberalism made a significant contribution to its early loss of interest in the older forms of missionary work.

This is more clearly seen when we remember that universalism and inclusivity are two of the central principles of liberalism. These principles stand fundamentally opposed to evangelism. The inner logic of the latter is clear enough: unless a person comes to explicit faith in Jesus Christ as Lord and Saviour he cannot enter the kingdom of heaven and therefore out of love for humanity and in obedience to its Lord, the Church must be engaged in the business of trying to bring as many as possible to the faith. How could it do anything less? But when you believe that no one is ultimately outside the kingdom and that all will be saved then what is the point of engaging in evangelism? Indeed you may be opposed to evangelism on the grounds that it is arrogant and imperialistic. This should not be surprising when we note that the current generation of liberals is hard at work trying to remove the very concept of "Lord" from the Christian vocabulary. The bottom line is that liberalism and evangelism are, along with the two religions they represent, mutually exclusive in principle and in practice. And liberal "inclusivity" ends where traditional/orthodox "exclusivity" begins.

3) New Religion: New Mission

When we turn to the history of missions in the last hundred years we can see how this has actually worked itself out in the life of the Church as the new religion entered its bloodstream. Liberals did not abandon mission as one might expect. However, as they often did with traditional concepts, they redefined it. In this case it is perhaps more true to say they refined it. In the nineteenth century many of those most concerned with evangelization were at the same time developing a strong social conscience, seeing the need for the reform of societal structures in order to alleviate suffering and injustice. Liberals found themselves attracted to this aspect of mission partly because it did not seem to require a supernaturalist view of reality. It was focused on the here and now instead of the possibilities of heaven and hell. Heaven and hell were made irrelevant, in effect, by the acceptance of universalism.

In fact, while all this was taking place around the turn of the century, liberals also were proclaiming the new dogma of "The Fatherhood of God and the Brotherhood of Man". While this slogan may look like a commonly accepted truth to most Christians, it is now clear that its proponents at the time meant it as an expression of universalism. Rather than meaning only that every human being was the special creation of the Almighty and thus a respected and equal part of the human family (a Biblical concept), it also embodied the idea that all of humanity automatically comprised the "Family of God" (not a Biblical idea). This fit hand in glove with the new way of defining mission as what became known as the "social gospel".

This development marked a shift towards seeing Christian mission predominately in terms of social justice. The incoming of the Kingdom of God was to be accomplished through changing social structures. To this enterprise liberals have brought a profound and admirable commitment. It helped that liberals of all stripes here found common ground. For one thing a common view of Jesus is not a necessary part of the agenda. There is no real need to talk about him very much at all except perhaps as a great teacher and example of how we are all to live. The message was not really about him. Instead it was about bricks and mortar, about politics and economics, about social sin rather than personal sin. This message found particular resonance, not so much with the teaching of Jesus, but with certain clear strains in the writings of the Old Testament prophets.

There is no doubt that the whole church owes a great debt to liberalism due to the way it has raised our consciousness in reference to social justice. The consistency and persistence exhibited in pursuing this goal have been remarkable if not inspirational. However it also needs to be said that wherever this approach to mission came to dominate, as it eventually did in the leadership of the ACC and much of mainstream Christianity in North America, the missionary zeal which had characterized the previous period of church history was quickly extinguished.

Odd as it may seem today it was this zeal that lay behind the very formation of the General Synod of the Anglican Church of Canada in 1893. It was partly a concern to facilitate the support of the missionary work in the North that originally motivated the Canadian dioceses to come together. The Church also had its own very active Missionary Society for years but this is no longer the case. The Society was upheld by the laudable efforts of its Women's Auxiliary, the old W.A. This has been replaced by the Anglican Church Women. In spite of this less focussed title many ACW groups continue to be missionary minded. It is also significant that the "Special Service for Missions", with its explicit prayers for the "evangelizing of the world" and the conversion of "the heathen", was removed from the Prayer Book in the revision of 1959.

Today the whole Canadian Church supports only a mere handful of full-time missionaries through the National Church's Department of World Mission. Missionaries, in the sense of those sent out to bring the Gospel of Jesus Christ to those who have had little or no opportunity to hear it before, are simply not part of the Church's official mission any longer. This is not to say that there is nothing good being accomplished in terms of our work with our overseas partners through the National Church, but the focus has shifted to short-term mission largely to do with the social gospel rather than winning the lost for Christ.

4) Conclusion: "B" Does Not Go Into "A"

Of course there still happen to be many thousands of Anglicans who vigorously disagree and are deeply offended by this change. To them the conversion of non-Christians is at the very heart of the Gospel and cannot be excluded without the denial of that Gospel. It is impossible to overstate their dismay when they realize that world evangelization, which they believe is the only real hope for humanity and the main reason for the existence of the church, is simply not a priority within the official structures of their own denomination. They are understandably alienated from the Department of

World Mission and find themselves supporting other unofficial mission agencies either within the Church (such as the South American Missionary Society) or on the outside (such as the Overseas Missionary Fellowship) who still make evangelism a priority. These patterns, however lamentable, are inevitable when two incompatible faiths share the same institution. If National Church bureaucrats as well as bishops are frustrated by the reluctance of many Anglicans to support mission through the official channels they can find a good part of the reason right here: the two religions have two differing concepts of mission. This is how deep our division runs.

This is why I speak "of decayed evangelism" in the Anglican Church of Canada. It is not that no evangelism is being done in the Anglican Church of Canada, but it is only being done by those of traditional/orthodox faith. Some parishes have enjoyed at least modest success in this area, especially those with a ministry to university students. Many Anglicans also took advantage of the fact that one of the most prominent Anglican evangelists of our generation, the Rev. Michael Green, spent considerable time in Canada recently as Professor of Evangelism at Regent College in Vancouver. Originally from England, he has now returned at the request of the Archbishop of Canterbury in order to assist in the task of evangelism in that country. It is perhaps an indication of where we are in Canada that he did not end up in a similar role here. There certainly remains much to be learned and applied in this area even among those who identify themselves as "evangelical" Anglicans. While they have the theology needed for evangelism they have not been doing a very good job, mostly because they have been preoccupied with secondary matters. If some have hoped that evangelical Anglicans would act as a kind of recruiting agency for the rest of the Church they have been disappointed. The whole Church needs to be mobilized for this task.

Clearly this will not be done as long as liberalism dominates the power structures of the denomination. Sadly the call of Lambeth to be engaged in "the primary task" of the Church in this Decade of Evangelism has fallen on deaf ears here in Canada. Instead the Church has abandoned the only remaining way for it to increase its membership just when it is needed the most. Not a good sign.

(c) SYMPTOM 3: The Falling Dollar (Reprise)

There are a number of ways in which the present and impending financial crisis in the Anglican Church of Canada can be linked to liberalism.

We have already seen that the membership decline in the denomination can be attributed in significant measure to liberalism. Fewer people means less money. Beyond this rather simple but all too accurate equation, some of the specific reasons for the membership decline help to explain the financial situation. The same reasons that have led persons to leave the Church also have dulled the motivation to give among many of those who are left. Those who are traditional/orthodox Christians will have a general unease about the direction the Church has been going. Liberalism's universalistic message lacks a note of urgency and even causes many to question its relevance. To these explanations one must add the fact that the aging membership (attributable in part to liberalism) contains many who are on fixed incomes and simply cannot increase their support.

Another major way in which liberalism has contributed to the financial woes of the Church is the fact that its general attitude to the authority of Scripture has effectively cut it off from the biblical solution: tithing. Liberals have sent the clear message that the Bible is not a reliable guide after all. It is full of errors and its teaching is culturally conditioned. So when attempts are made to promote the biblical tithe of 10% of income (or the "modern" tithe of 5%) one can be excused for wondering why this particular teaching of the bible is so enthusiastically endorsed. One might even be tempted to ascribe the real motive not to a desire to promote a biblical lifestyle but to the fact that Church officials know that if Anglicans did begin to tithe their budget troubles would be over and none of their programs would be threatened. It should be noted, as a simple observable fact, that Christians who live in a denominational atmosphere that upholds the traditional/orthodox view of the Scriptures as the Word of God have a much greater tendency to tithe than those who do not.

Finally, reference must be made to what may be the most compelling reason to link liberalism to the falling dollar. In a day when there is increasing competition for the charitable dollar people must be highly motivated to give to a particular cause. Earlier, in Chapter Two (see "A Complex Superiority", p. 31), I explored the ways in which a serious division has developed between laity and the clergy elite of the Anglican Church of Canada. This has resulted at the very least in a serious communications problem and at most a sense of alienation from the leadership. Certainly there is widespread disinterest. In such a context it would only be natural to expect lukewarm financial support for programs perceived as coming down from on high. As the editor of the Anglican Journal recently put it:

> Cynicism and a distrust of authority are blamed for much of the reluctance at the grassroots level to contribute to the national church's coffers. And this reluctance is taking place at a time when the national church is being asked to do more with less. (Feb. 1996)

To some extent this "cynicism and distrust of authority" is the product of our time. Look at modern politics, for example. The elitism evident in the Anglican Church is, as I will argue, to a significant degree the direct product of liberalism. Thus it is liberalism itself which must bear a large part of the responsibility for the current financial crisis. The people are just not buying what liberalism is selling.

(d) SYMPTOM 4: Indecent Disorder (Reprise)

We must now return to those indications of the considerable confusion in the life of the Anglican Church of Canada in order to show that much of this "indecent disorder" can be linked to the new religion of liberalism.

1) Uncommon Prayer (Reprise)

As we saw under this title in Chapter Two (p. 21), the Anglican Church of Canada has, since the arrival of the "liturgical renewal" movement, moved into a time of ever-multiplying liturgies. This has resulted in a radically altered ecclesiastical landscape, a territory unfamiliar to most Anglicans and unnerving to many. It is now our task to see how much all of this is due to liberalism.

(A) As the People Understandeth

It must be said at the outset that the call for liturgical revision itself cannot be blamed on liberalism. Although many Anglicans appear to have forgotten this fact, the Prayer Book itself arose out of a deep conviction of the English reformers that worship was to be conducted "...in such a tongue as the people understandeth." (Article XXIV) While at the time this was directed at the Latin mass, the principle remains that for Anglicans worship must be in the language of the worshipper. This leads inevitably to a second principle: because language changes over time and place it is necessary for liturgy to be revised in order to reflect this reality. As the Preface to the "revision" of 1662 puts it:

> ...it is reasonable, that upon weighty and important considerations, according to the various exigency of times and occasions, such changes and alterations should be made therein, as to those that are in place of authority should from time to time seem either necessary or expedient. (BCP, p. 719)

If you have difficulty understanding this passage that is because it was written in the English of that time and reflects a vocabulary, phrasing and structure that is much different than our language. The liturgy which was produced in that era, the Book of Common Prayer, was a "contemporary" liturgy. It speaks the language of the day. It is certain that the Reformers would have been surprised to discover that their spiritual descendents were still worshipping in this language three hundred years later, given that English had changed considerably over that time. So it is a good and Anglican thing to revise liturgy, especially with a view to ensuring that worship is conducted in a language that is fully understood by the people.

In this sense, therefore the desire for "contemporary rites" is part of our heritage, even if it had been seriously neglected for a time. While this authenticates part of what has happened over the last thirty years, it fails to explain why the Canadian Church has moved away from the tradition of "common prayer". It is one thing to insist on worshipping in contemporary language; it is quite another to endorse an endless multiplying of liturgies for various communities within the Church. This moves us beyond mere language and into the realm of theology and here we find, not surprisingly, that liberalism is at the centre of this development.

(B) Many Gospels, Many Liturgies

The problem is that liberalism cannot be contained in any one liturgy. Just as it is by nature forever changing and without boundaries so also is its liturgical expression. Liberalism's tendency towards fragmentization was explored in Chapter Three (see especially "Free-Falling Apart", p. 59ff.). It was pointed out there as well that the 1985 Book of Alternative Services (BAS), although in form dramatically different than the Book of Common Prayer, was, in reality, a moderately liberal revision from the theological point of view. However it was soon obsolete as liberalism continued to spin off in various directions and its newer variations experimented with liturgies which more fully reflected these trends. In this context the ideal of "common prayer" itself became obsolete.

To be specific, the liberal elite soon began to reflect the cultural relativism (inclusivity), radical feminism, and pro-gay agenda of its secular counterpart. As it did it found the BAS, not to mention the largely bypassed BCP, hopelessly out of date. Given an atmosphere which encouraged liturgical innovation, it wasn't long before experimentation was in progress on each of these fronts. In a motion that was tabled at the last General Synod the Church was asked to open the door to liturgies for the blessing of "monogamous same-gender unions". At a clergy conference in central Canada the participants confessed themselves believers in "...God, Mother-Father spirit". This same "creed", in what was supposed to be a Christian service, does not mention any belief in Jesus Christ, let alone the Trinity. A liturgy used at a private school in eastern Canada simply omitted the Creed and the Gloria and refused to pray in the name of Jesus Christ at all. In fact the only reference to Jesus was in the prayer of consecration itself where he apparently is still unavoidable. From this perspective the BAS is obviously much too traditional and increasingly inappropriate.

Those communities within the Church that have arrived at these new understandings of the faith are naturally demanding the right to worship as they see fit. Liberalism, as part of its commitment to cultural diversity, cannot but agree to these demands. It seeks to promote the idea that each distinctive group within society should be able to set its own agenda free of the imposition of the values of the larger society. So liberalism, largely because of its inability to set boundaries, creates both a multiplicity of liturgies and the atmosphere that deliberately welcomes these developments. It therefore comes as no surprise that General Synod has agreed to the production of supplementary eucharistic rites for feminists, evangelicals, aboriginals and other groups. This is just cultural diversity. It can never lead to common prayer.

Those evangelicals who, in resisting the BAS, insisted on composing contemporary liturgies for their own parochial use have also contributed to the demise of common prayer. However, they did not start out in this direction. If the compilers of the BAS had been willing to make a few key changes and include in the book at least one eucharistic prayer (out of six) that clearly reflected a Prayer Book theology things would have been different. In spite of much petitioning from the evangelical side of the Church this was not done and some, at least, resorted to doing their own thing. They felt, not for the first time, excluded by the liberal church. Not having another option, it was every man for himself. Ironically, if they had been included from the start they undoubtedly would have been content with the BAS and would now be its staunchest defenders! Certainly, in the light of what liberals were soon doing, the changes evangelicals (and others) requested were moderate indeed.

Liberalism, then, is the real driving force behind the current proliferation of experimental liturgies. Because liberalism is forever fragmenting in a process that knows no boundaries, so also is the liturgical innovation it has spawned. Liberalism brings division, always and everywhere. It has bequeathed us with the era of "uncommon prayer".

2) Hymns and Hers (Reprise)

(A) Introduction: Only Making It Worse

One of the signs of the lack of unity in the Anglican Church of Canada is the increasingly wide diversity of worship music that congregations are using. It must be stressed at the outset that this cannot seriously be blamed on liberalism. Rather it is largely a function of liturgical renewal on the one hand and an explosion of contemporary worship music on the other.

If liberalism is not the actual cause of our division in this aspect of our worship, it does make a significant contribution to its depth, making it doubly difficult to restore common praise to the denomination. With the publication of the proposed new hymn book the Church will be entering an era in which a significant proportion of its members will actually be unable to bring themselves to sing "the hymns of the church" for doctrinal reasons.

(B) Lots to Choose From: Contemporary Hymns

Now it is true that there is a bewildering variety of contemporary Christian music. It is important to understand, however, that almost all of this is written by and for traditional/orthodox Christians anxious to worship in contemporary language and idiom. It is a truly grassroots ecumenical movement. Broadly labeled "renewal" music it spreads through a thousand different channels with no one central focal point. Congregational worship leaders can tap into this stream in a number of ways, often through direct exposure at conferences and larger gatherings. As a result any one parish will have its own selection of new music which will vary considerably from its neighbour depending on what appeals to both leadership and congregation.

Within all this variety, however, there is a clear commitment to the traditional/orthodox faith. It explicitly proclaims the Trinitarian God, Father, Son and Holy Spirit and well as such doctrines as the deity and bodily resurrection of Jesus. As a result there is thus a substantial unity underlying all this diversity rooted in the core doctrines of catholic Christianity. The differences between parishes who use such music are more matters of style and taste than of substance. In fact much of this music comes out of a similar mold. Visitors familiar with at least some the contemporary music would quickly feel at home anywhere.

This is not to imply that all those of traditional/orthodox faith have enthusiastically embraced renewal music. Far from it. The new music comes attached to a more informal and personalized style of worship which is not attractive to many Anglicans. In addition, some find that much of the new music does not reflect the theological depth of more traditional hymns. Indeed, many congregations who do use the newer music also continue to employ the older hymns for just this reason. Both sides in this debate have something valid to say to each other. Thus, although there is some division within the traditional/orthodox camp over this aspect of worship, it is not a matter of first importance. There is an underlying commitment to biblical theology on the part of both sides.

(C) One Part Harmony: The New Hymn Book

Liberals, on the other hand, seem to be going in a completely other direction. They often appear largely uninterested in the personal, even intimate, relationship with God expressed in renewal music and at odds with what they see as the patriarchal and exclusivist religion of traditional hymnody. They have taken to revising the latter and pretty well ignoring the former. The exception to this would be a modest body of folk style hymns, often best supported by acoustic guitar. Many of these reflect an interest in peace, justice and social issues. Compared to renewal music, however, this could in no way be described as popular, arising out of a groundswell of grassroots demand.

It is almost exclusively this liberal perspective which seems to lie behind the hymn book now being put together under the Hymn Book Task Force. It is not a compilation of congregational favourites. The Task Force told General Synod that although it had worked through the texts of the proposed hymns for the book and had assigned tunes to most of them, this aspect of the work was not yet completed. Published reports indicate that it contains no renewal music at all. Most of the hymns included are in traditional music styles from the 17th and 18th centuries as well as the Victorian and Edwardian periods. Paradoxically, then, the tunes for the hymns in this "new" hymn book are predominately traditional! But the same cannot be said of the text. As was noted in Chapter Two those older hymns which are retained have seen extensive revision and some of the newer ones introduce concepts and imagery that have never before appeared in the authorized hymnody of the Christian church. It only needs pointing out here that almost all of these come out of the understanding of the new religion of liberalism and are an offense to traditional/orthodox Christians.

It is only liberals, many now embracing radical feminism, who desire to introduce "inclusive" language in reference to God, even to the point of goddess worship. It is only liberals who want to replace "Father, Son and Holy Spirit" with "Creator, Redeemer and Sustainer" and who avoid as much as possible referring to the fact that God is our Father or that Jesus is a man. It is only liberals who shy away from patriarchal and hierarchical terms for God, especially "Lord" and "King". It is only liberals who are shy about Satan and squeamish about sin. It is only liberals who are embarrassed over the triumph of Christ and his Church.

Therefore many of these new liberal hymns and revisions of older hymns cannot be sung in good conscience by traditional./orthodox Christians. It is not merely a matter of taste. It is difficult to say what is going to happen when a Synod opens with "Womb of life and source of being". Traditional/orthodox believers certainly will not sing such words. Some may even feel the need to walk out of such worship.

Liberals will find this difficult to accept because they have, after all, been singing words to which they objected for years! Why can't the other side simply do the same? But, as we have seen, the other side has a completely different understanding of revelation, language and symbol which makes it more difficult to inject new meaning into old words or to sing with one's fingers crossed. This is one of the places where we can clearly see the limits of liberal inclusivism. Here those of traditional/orthodox faith are excluded. The fundamental division of the Anglican Church into its two incompatible religions is painfully evident. Perhaps the compilers of the new hymn book were right after all when they omitted "Thy hand, O God, has guided":

> And we, shall we be faithless?
> Shall hearts fail, hands hang down?
> Shall we evade the conflict,
> And cast away our crown?
> Not so: in God's deep counsels
> Some better thing is stored;
> We will maintain, unflinching,
> One Church, one Faith, one Lord. (verse 5)

How can we sing such a song?

3) Curriculum, Curricula (Reprise)

What is the relationship of liberalism to the evident disarray in Christian education within the Anglican Church of Canada? It will be recalled that this area shares in the general disunity that one finds at almost every level of Church life.

As I have argued elsewhere, liberalism is by nature a fragmentizing agent. It knows no boundaries and is in constant flux. Even its emphasis upon experience takes it in the same direction, into expressions that are as varied as the experience of persons is varied. While it is tempting to draw a direct line from the nature of liberalism to the fragmentization of the Church's educative efforts, things are not quite so simple.

For one thing such an explanation fails to account for the wide variety of approaches to this subject even among those Anglicans who are traditional/orthodox Christians. It could be maintained that this phenomenon is at least indirectly the result of liberalism to the extent that it led to both the introduction of the "New Curriculum" and its rejection by the grassroots in the mid-sixties. Indeed, when the histories are written it may be that the New Curriculum will be identified as the first official endorsement of the new way of thinking. As a replacement for the aging but thoroughly orthodox General Board of Religious Education (G.B.R.E.) curriculum it failed to attract the same wide usage, thus creating a vacuum. Many parishes were not happy with the revised denominational curriculum and felt it necessary to look elsewhere. As they were basically on their own they naturally ended up in going in a number of different directions. More liberal parishes were also left in a vacuum when the New Curriculum was withdrawn with no replacement. They too had to scramble.

If the old G.B.R.E. curriculum had been brought up to date while retaining its traditional/orthodox perspective it would perhaps have continued to provide a denominational Sunday School curriculum that was widely acceptable and therefore more viable. At the same time it could have provided the foundation for a stronger sense of unity within the Church. But this would have left liberals on the outside looking in instead of the other way around. Again we have a "for instance" of the incompatibility of the two religions now in the Church.

As far as the issues of baptismal and confirmation preparation are concerned, it must be admitted that the smorgasbord of ideas is endemic to liberal and traditional/orthodox alike. There are good and sufficient reasons for the present turmoil swirling around the general issue of Christian initiation which have nothing to do with liberalism. It will be impossible to resolve them until a reformed Church emerges with its doctrinal foundation secure. It will then be able to address these issues from a common perspective and, as a result, bring some order out of chaos. At that time the whole question of adult Christian education can also be addressed. For now we can expect only constant turmoil and continued division.

(e) SYMPTOM 5: A Complex Superiority (Reprise)

As was noted when this subject was first addressed, clericalism, the dominance of the clergy, has been a feature of church life almost from the beginning. This is due in large measure to the very nature of the church and is to some extent inescapable and even good. The historic division between the clergy and the laity has, however, reached dangerous proportions in the Anglican Church of Canada. Much of this can also be traced to the presence of the liberal religion in the denomination.

1) Gloria Goes to the Source

Perhaps the best way to try to understand this is to follow an imaginary seminarian as she proceeds through the educative process on the way to ordination. As we do so we will discover the basic reason why the clergy have become so alienated from the laity. I must stress at the outset that while the following description reflects a typical experience it does not represent the situation in all our schools or the positions of all their faculty members. Having said that, let us call our student "Gloria" and assume that she is a "cradle" Anglican from a city parish who has felt "the call". Perhaps this is a response to a conversion experience as a teenager after which she augmented her Sunday School knowledge by enthusiastically reading and studying her Bible. After four years of university she arrives on the doorstep of an Anglican theological college eager to acquire a sure foundation by means of a thorough exploration of the faith of the Church.

What Gloria gets is a baptism of fire. Almost every assumption she has brought with her will be brought into serious question. By the end of three years she will, unless she shows great determination and courage, emerge with a radically altered understanding of the faith. The College, typically, is deeply committed to the kind of liberalism outlined in the previous chapter and is in fact the major point at which this new religion is introduced into the bloodstream of the Church. Gloria's Sunday School faith and her "uncritical" reading of the Scriptures will be under constant and direct attack. She will be informed that no truly modern person could take the Bible at face value, as she has always done. Assured that all mainstream scholars concur, Gloria is then initiated into the mysteries of JPED, pseudepigraphy, demythologization and the entire program of "modern biblical criticism" (cf. "A Brave New Worldview", p. 56ff.)

She will quickly realize that from this point of view her simple understanding of the faith cannot be sustained and as a result she is plunged into a traumatic and painful crisis of faith. This might come to a head, for example, when she is exposed to the scholarly opinion that the accounts of Jesus's resurrection appearances in the four Gospels are hopelessly contradictory and certainly cannot provide any support to the idea of a bodily resurrection (which modern people cannot accept in any event). What really happened, she is informed, is that the early church somehow came to have an experience of the "risen Lord" in their midst and these stories of the empty tomb and appearances were written later in order to try to express this spiritual reality in concrete terms understandable to the people of the day. Ill-prepared for this assault on what she had always believed, Gloria is faced with either following what Mrs. Augustine had so faithfully taught her in Sunday School or what she was now learning through the authorized and sophisticated teachers of the Church. She might well identify with this quotation from a recent newspaper interview with an Anglican seminary student:

> If you want spirituality, don't go to a seminary. They turn you upside down and inside out and some of us survive and some of us don't. Seminary is not what I expected and not what a lot of others perceive it to be...If you go even not half sure of your faith, you won't make it through. (Saint John Times-Globe, August 2, 1996)

The seminary experience almost seems designed to destroy the simple faith of those students still holding to such an outmoded and intellectually unacceptable religion.

Just as Gloria is feeling the foundation of her old faith begin to crumble she is then introduced to the new faith, liberalism, in whatever form or forms it is taking on campus. The culture of seminary life brings powerful pressure on her to conform to one of these. The current models available to her would include radical feminism (up to and including goddess worship and witchcraft), liberation theology (leftist political agenda) and eco-justice (environmentalism). The first of these seems to have the greatest following at the present time and this perhaps explains the wide acceptance of homosexual practice within some of these institutions.

In the face of all this Gloria may well decide that she has had enough and just drop out. If she continues she will have three options. First of all she may quietly resist the new teaching. I say quietly because vocal, active opposition to the reigning versions is not tolerated well and can lead to much unseemly confrontation. After all, one's whole view of life is at stake. Secondly, she can go with the flow and convert to the new religion altogether. Lastly, she will remain unsure of her beliefs but continue on in her studies in the hope that it will all get sorted out eventually.

Whichever option she selects it is unlikely that it will form any barrier to her being ordained. She will have to commit herself to "conform to the doctrine...of the Anglican Church of Canada" but this is carefully left undefined and it is commonly understood to include any of the liberal varieties as well as traditional/orthodox Christianity. The only belief she will have to affirm in a specific way is the ordination of women, which for her should not be a problem! Even if she had doubts about this "doctrine" she could still affirm it in good conscience. After all, she has learned that the doctrine of the Church is always open to various interpretations. The belief in the ordination of women, like others before it, needn't be taken in its crude literal sense. Perhaps it could be taken as our culture's particular expression of the underlying truth that God has called both women and men to serve humanity. In the latter sense it can then be safely affirmed.

Let us presume that Gloria chooses the middle option and buys into the liberal religion. Imagine the task she will face in the parish. Here she is likely to be faced with a congregation in which many have the same Sunday School faith she has left behind. Every Sunday large portions of raw Scripture are read to them and then she has to get up in the pulpit and try to expound a message that does not easily arise out of the text. She has been ill-equipped by seminary to provide her listeners with a way to move from where they are to where she is. Fortunately they are predisposed to defer to her greater understanding of the faith She is a clergyperson, after all. But still she is distanced from them by her training and her faith journey. They hear her words but are baffled by her theological terminology. It sounds vaguely familiar but it lacks clear meaning. In this context any changes she feels are necessary are often perceived as imposed, arising out of her agenda, not theirs. She and they are in separate worlds. At best her socialist politics and radical feminism may be tolerated as the typical product of the ivory tower not of the real world. What is she to do as the pastor in such a situation?

One thing is almost certain. Gloria will not embark on a program to encourage the uninstructed reading or study of the Bible. She will not do this because she knows, consciously or unconsciously, that the reading of the Scriptures in an "uncritical" fashion, in the pre-modern belief that takes its words in their everyday sense, will lead only to an affirmation of the Sunday School faith she has rejected as obsolete for contemporary Christians. She is certainly not opposed to the reading of the Bible but is acutely aware that, in order for it to be properly understood, it must be interpreted by someone who comes from the perspective of modern critical scholarship. For most parishes that leaves only one person who is qualified. Guess who!

What Gloria may not fully realize, however, is that *her old Sunday School faith bears an uncanny resemblance to catholic Christianity.* As I have argued in Chapter Three (p. 50ff.) the catholic faith arises out of the understanding of the Bible as God's Word written. It is the final authority. If it says that Jesus rose bodily from the grave and lives forevermore at the right hand of the Father then that is what Christians are to believe and nothing else. End of argument. This is taking it at face value following the normal rules of grammar. Once this way of approaching Scripture is abandoned so also will catholic Christianity be abandoned. What this logic has dictated, history has now fulfilled.

2) Closing the Good Book

Ironically, the Anglican Church began with an attempt to go in exactly the opposite direction. The English Reformers deliberately set about to put the Bible *back into* the hands of the average believer. It was to be loosed from the fetters imposed by those who had distorted its teachings and had forbidden its use. Let it be read and believed by one and all! For them the reading of the Bible in its plain ordinary sense was the greatest source of spiritual life that God has provided to his people. It is his Word written, after all. It was to be translated from the Latin into the common tongue and placed in every parish church. Archbishop Thomas Cranmer, the composer of much of the Prayer Book, had this to say:

> Unto a Christian man, there can be nothing either more necessary or profitable, than the knowledge of Holy Scripture; forasmuch as in it is contained God's true word, setting forth his glory, and also man's duty. And there is no truth nor doctrine, necessary for our justification and everlasting salvation, but that is, or may be, drawn from that fountain and well of truth. Therefore as many as be desirous to enter into the right and perfect way unto God, must apply their minds to know Holy Scripture;
> And as drink is pleasant to them that be dry, and meat to them that be hungry; so is the reading, hearing, searching, and studying of Holy Scripture...

> And, on the other side, nothing more darkeneth Christ and the glory of God, nor bringeth in more blindness and all kinds of vices, that doth the ignorance of God's word. (The Homilies, Book I:1)

So we have come full circle. At one time our Church recognized and exploited the connection between the straightforward reading of the Bible by ordinary people and spiritual vitality. *Modern critical scholarship has taken the Bible away from the Church just as effectively as the Roman Church had done by the late middle ages*. This time around no one is actually forbidden to read the Bible. But in a number of different ways parishioners are told that its true meaning lies behind what it says on the surface and that it takes a special knowledge to be able to access that meaning. They are told this by many within the clergy-elite, the ones to whom they look for spiritual guidance. In Anglican homes the Bible has typically become a closed book, literally as well as figuratively. The result is a biblically illiterate laity and a confused, moribund Church. It is no accident.

There is a great sadness in this. Those like Gloria who have chosen to follow the liberal religion have not only distanced themselves from many of their parishioners, they have sealed themselves off from their past, a past which points the way, the only way, to another reformation and a yet more glorious future.

(iii) An Alarming Conclusion

No doubt I have made my point. But let me make it again in case you missed it! Liberalism by its very nature has been and continues to be the basic reason for the troubles that afflict the Anglican Church of Canada. Its attempt to present a new message in the old words has resulted in misunderstanding and confusion among the rank and file. It creates disorder because it is fundamentally disorderly. Membership decline and financial woes are its constant companions. Incompatible with the very idea of evangelism, it has proven itself incapable of attracting significant numbers of new adherents. This is what liberalism is and this is what it does.

Do I sound like an alarmist? Is my vision is narrow and false, distorted by anger, prejudice, ignorance and fear? I am content to let my readers be the judge of that. But I have come to the conviction that liberalism is not just another option within the spectrum of Christian truth. It is not merely the subject of polite conversation over a glass of sherry. It is a deadly enemy of Christ and his Church. Surely *someone* has to sound the alarm. Who else but an alarmist?

> The word of the LORD came to me: "Son of man, speak to your countrymen and say to them; 'When I bring the sword against a land, and the people of the land choose one of their men and make him their

watchman, and he sees the sword coming against the land and blows the trumpet to warn the people, then if anyone hears the trumpet but does not take the warning and the sword comes and takes his life, his blood will be on his own head. If he had taken warning, he would have saved himself. But if the watchman sees the sword coming and does not blow the trumpet to warn the people and the sword comes and takes the life of one of them, that man will be taken away because of his sin, but I will hold the watchman accountable for his blood.'

"Son of man, I have made you a watchman for the house of Israel; so hear the word I speak and give them warning from me..." (Ezekiel 33:1-7)

CHAPTER FIVE

Out of the Closet and Into the Abyss

"For there is nothing hidden that will not be disclosed, and nothing concealed that will not be known or brought out into the open. Therefore consider carefully how you will listen." (Luke 8:17-18a)

(i) The Issue to End All Issues?

(a) Introduction: Betting the Farm

Sooner or later, given the underlying division of the Anglican Church of Canada into two incompatible religions, there was bound to be an issue which would force this uncomfortable truth out into the open. For a number of reasons it is apparent that the crucial battle between liberals and traditional/orthodox supporters will probably be over morality. For a number of reasons it has been possible for many Anglicans to change their belief system without bringing us to the point of open division. In the previous generations liberals simply adopted conventional morality but eventually their new attitude to the Bible was applied to its ethical teachings as well as its theology. This was bound to force matters more out into the open. You can switch the meaning of your theological terms and not greatly disturb the status quo. However, change your understanding of "adultery" and someone is bound to notice! Probably your spouse!

As almost every Anglican knows, the critical moral question now before us is that of the acceptability of homosexual behaviour in the Christian community. Those on both sides appear willing to "bet the farm" because each properly sees this issue as symbolic of its whole point of view. That is why there can be no compromise and no surrender. To do so would mean not just changing one's mind about this issue but about one's whole approach to the Christian faith as well. This is what is at stake. The outcome will quite literally affect the entire future direction of the Church.

(b) Liberation: The Liberal Imperative

From the liberal point of view the question of the full acceptance of the homosexual "lifestyle", including the ordination of practicing homosexuals and the blessing of same-sex couples, is merely a matter of justice, liberation, and inclusion. We have already noted that these themes are dominant in liberalism. Homosexual persons have clearly suffered at the hands of an oppressive straight society, some physically attacked and even killed. They have not been allowed to be themselves but have been forced to hide their sexual orientation in order to function within that society. Recent years have seen many of them "come out of the closet" and some have militantly demanded that they be granted their "right" to have their sexuality accepted on a par with heterosexuality at all levels. Their cause has been taken up by the cultural elite, especially those on the left. It is socialism's agenda, as has been observed, that is often incorporated into theological liberalism. Many priests, liberal and otherwise, have found homosexuals in their congregations and have come to appreciate their gifts within the life of the Church as well their pain at being denied full participation.

All of the major themes of liberalism converge on this issue. Experience has taught that homosexuals are not such terrible people after all. They are as good and as human as the rest of us, hardly the degenerates of popular mythology. For liberals the negative things the Bible has to say about practicing homosexuals must be set alongside our own contemporary experience, remembering that the true nature of the Bible itself forces us to pick and choose from its teachings. Furthermore, homosexuals are seeking liberation, the freedom to be themselves. Nothing could be closer to the liberal heart. And here we are in a Church which makes them into second class citizens even in the unlikely event that they are welcomed at all. On what basis can they continue to be excluded? It is a shameful thing, from this perspective, that the Church is not prepared to reach out and fully welcome this oppressed minority, some of whom are occupying its pews and its pulpits. For these and other reasons, the full acceptance of practicing homosexuals has become a non-negotiable item on the liberal agenda. Any other stand would contradict their twin commitments to experience as the ultimate guide and to liberation as the ultimate goal.

This conclusion is illustrated and reinforced by recent comments by one of the leading liberal bishops, the Right Reverend Michael Ingham of Vancouver. He has openly declared his hope that the Church will "...soon allow parishes and dioceses to choose whether they want to bless same-sex unions...". In a front page article in the November 1996 issue of the

"Anglican Journal" he clearly expresses his eagerness and determination to proceed in this direction. He also, however, acknowledges the possibility of major schism (outright organizational division) over the issue. Bishop Ingham goes on to say that "...most other bishops find themselves on the 'horns of a dilemma' of preaching the Gospel [which, for him, demands the supporting of same-sex unions] and keeping the unity of the Church...". He then reveals that the House of Bishops is deeply divided on this issue and that some bishops are still seeking consensus. Bishop Ingham is clearly of the opinion that this is not possible and that the way out of the dilemma is for those who still hold to the traditional/orthodox point of view to change their minds as he himself has done.

He seems confident that this will happen eventually but one is left with the impression that he will not wait too much longer for the Church to give its permission. After all, for him, this is part of the Gospel and it is only natural to expect that he puts a higher priority on the Gospel than upon the unity of the Church. Unfortunately for the latter, the exact same attitude can be expected from those on the other side of the question. Both sides are prepared to "go to the wall". It is not a pretty picture.

(c) Redemption: The Traditional/Orthodox Imperative

There are some on both sides of this question that see it merely as an extension of the previous debates in the Church over divorce and remarriage and the ordination of women. From this point of view hope remains that some kind of accommodation can be reached here as well. While there is some truth to this position, it would be a serious mistake to assume too much similarity between this debate and those of the past. For one thing, the issue of homosexuality is a clear-cut case of morality rather than a question of order in the Church. This raises the stakes considerably. For another, on the previous issues the traditional/orthodox camp was divided pro and con. This had the effect of limiting outright opposition to a relatively small section of the Church. Many also recognized that the Biblical evidence in reference to the previous debates was ambiguous and could be legitimately seen as supportive of both sides. This made compromise and accommodation possible even when one personally felt others to be in error. *It cannot be stressed enough that this is not the case in the matter of homosexuality.*

Traditional/orthodox believers in the ACC are, with very few exceptions, at one in their opposition to the acceptance of homosexual practice as anything less than contrary to God's will and thus sinful. They are convinced that the Scripture relevant to this issue is both clear and unequivocal. Because these Anglicans are committed to the authority of the Bible in matters of faith and practice any stand taken contrary to this by the General Synod or by the House of Bishops will put them into an impossibly awkward position. They would then be part of a Church which, for the first time, had officially departed from the Scriptures. For them it would be as if the Trinity itself had been officially denied. The Church would finally have put itself over the Bible. This is the real issue. Homosexual practice is surely fairly low on any scale of sins but that is not the point. Accepting it would mean that the ACC had finally taken the step many have feared it would ultimately take, given the dominance of liberalism in its ranks. It could have been taken in reference to any other clearly biblical doctrine or practice. In taking such action the ACC would, in the eyes of its traditional/orthodox members, officially abandon the view of Scripture and its authority which has been the theological foundation of the catholic church from the beginning.

This foundation has already been abandoned by the liberal wing of the Church. Once the Church is deliberately willing to set aside the traditional understanding of Scripture there will be no further barriers to the official adoption of the whole liberal agenda. *What we believe and practice as a Church will be determined by the current consensus. It will be revealed by a majority vote in the General Synod and will become the "truth" no matter what Scripture says and what the church has always taught.* Already some liberal ethicists are warm to the acceptance of pre-marital sex and certain forms of adultery. With experience as the guide there is literally no telling in what direction the Church will go and there is no way to direct it except through the use of raw political power.

This is not the kind of Church in which many traditional/orthodox Christians could feel comfortable for very long. While the facade of the "official doctrine of the Church" remained in place it was possible for them to function as Anglicans with a reasonable degree of integrity. For many years they have been at odds with what has been going on behind the scenes but have been content to get on with the job of ministry, letting others involve themselves in the politics of the Church. Those others have tended to be more liberal, pre-disposed to see the Kingdom as a matter of social and political action and so drawn to get more involved in church government and bureaucracy. Therefore it is partly through its own neglect that the traditional/orthodox camp finds itself on the outside looking in as far as power in the Church is concerned. Now, with the possibility of a serious departure from the faith on the horizon its sense of alienation is exacerbated by an almost overwhelming sense of powerlessness. This is a recipe for mass defection.

There are several other reasons to think that the acceptance of homosexual practice will result in many feeling they have no option but to leave the ACC. For some it will be a simple case of not wanting to be part of a Church that is officially affirming as right and good what they consider to be sinful. It is one thing to know that some in the Church have departed from the faith. It is quite another to realize the Church itself has done so. This would be too much. Others would see in such acceptance the official abandonment of Scripture as the rule of faith and this would cast a serious shadow over any claim of the ACC to be part of the church universal. Certainly most would agree that it had little claim to be the same Church as Cranmer and Hooker and the Book of Common Prayer. Furthermore, many of the leaders within the traditional/orthodox camp are openly saying that they would have to leave. Even the Rev. John Stott, one of the most respected of these leaders worldwide, has recently said that he could not long remain in a Church that blessed homosexual practice. This is especially significant because Stott has heretofore dedicated his formidable talents to convincing disaffected evangelicals to stay in the Anglican Church and work for reform from the inside.

For those of traditional/orthodox persuasion involved in pastoral ministry the official endorsement of homosexual practice will prove to be a difficult impediment if not an impossible burden. Following the practice of our Lord, they are working out of a system that calls for loving and accepting the homosexual person while at the same time recognizing his lifestlye as sinful. Truly loving a homosexual person involves encouraging him to repent of the sin that is besetting him. Only in this way can he be restored to a proper relationship with God and grow in grace. It is same path that all us sinners must take. It is the path we take in Holy Baptism. It is the Gospel path. To hold this view and at the same time not call for repentance is actually an *uncaring* act. Authentic love for someone results in taking actions perceived to be in his or her best interest. Persisting in sin is to impede and eventually destroy one's relationship with God. From this perspective there is a very real fear for the eternal souls of those who might be confirmed in their sin by official Church policy. Continuing to belong to and even represent an organization that endorses sin is intolerable. It is a pact with the devil.

It must also be said that many Anglicans are still convinced that homosexual practice is often (though not always) the result of and results in unhealthy and broken relationships. Study after study has shown this to be the case but we are now asked by those advocating acceptance to put all this aside, to bury our therapeutic heads in the sand and pretend it does not exist. Much suffering is going to remain unaddressed and pathological patterns will be perpetuated and made worse by official endorsement. Further, it will be exceedingly difficult to continue to uphold the position that homosexual practice is sin when your denomination declares otherwise. How can you call for homosexuals to renounce their lifestyle when the Church in which one serves is ordaining them? How can you counsel them toward healing when the Church says they are healthy? Finally, how can any sense of unity among the ranks of the clergy be retained when one parish has an openly gay couple sharing the rectorship while in the next parish such relationships are just as openly proclaimed to be sinful?

Given what happened in the case of the ordination of women it is certain that such open proclamation would be actively discouraged by the Church. At first those clergy who objected to the ordination of women were permitted to continue in their ministries protected by the so-called "conscience clause". The provision of such a measure was a key element in getting General Synod's approval of the ordination of women in the first place. It recognized the right of persons to disassociate themselves from the ministry of ordained women while at the same time committing them not to obstruct such ministry. Eventually, however, the conscience clause was removed, effectively making only one view possible in any public sense. It is now understood that the Church will only ordain those who accept the ordination of women. In this way the opposing view will be eventually eliminated from the Church.

In this context it is extremely unlikely that those who are opposed to the ordination of practicing homosexuals would ever accept the imposition of a "conscience clause". It would be clearly seen as an unstable solution that would eventually have only one outcome: the eventual elimination of all opposition to the position adopted by the General Synod. Everyone on both sides of the question, because of recent history, would be unwilling to see a conscience clause as an acceptable compromise.

(d) Conclusion: An Accident Waiting To Happen

Two trains are heading toward each other on the same track. Transfixed by the horror of what is about to happen we stare out at the scene immobile, helpless, as the disaster approaches. Is there not a button we can push or a switch we can throw? Where is a good alarmist when you need one?

(ii) The National Study Program on Homosexuality

(a) Introduction: One Train At a Time, Please

It is not as if the Church hasn't done anything about this issue. It comes with a history. Part of that history is the Study Program it provided for use in parishes. There are a number of excellent reasons for giving it our careful consideration. For one thing it is obviously the chosen vessel to guide the discussion of this issue in the Anglican Church of Canada. For another, it represents an almost perfect example of the decidedly liberal bias which has marked most of the official efforts of the Church for many years. It is a classic case of a sincere attempt to be inclusive which actually ends up excluding and demoralizing those who do not share liberal assumptions. From this point of view it can serve well to illustrate the argument made earlier on just this point ("The Exclusion of Orthodoxy", p. 71). In this sense it is an acknowledgment that there really can only be one train on the track.

(b) Historical Background

Until very recently the shared teaching of the Anglican Church of Canada on the subject of homosexuality was that of the whole Christian church throughout its history: the practice is a sin. In 1979 the bishops issued "guidelines" which held that persons of homosexual orientation could be ordained but had to promise that they would not engage in sexual practice (just like any non-married person). Some saw this as the beginning of a change in position because it did not require the homosexual person to acknowledge that such practice was, in fact, sinful. Be that as it may, the statement was based on the helpful insight that made a distinction between "orientation" and "practice". This statement was re-affirmed in1991, while in that same year the Human Rights Unit of the National Church produced the resource, "Our Stories, Your Story" in an attempt to enable the whole church to hear the voices of gay and lesbian people. The General Synod of 1992 called for a study of homosexuality and for a report to be submitted to the 1995 General Synod. Eventually a Task Force on Homosexuality and Homosexual Relationships was formed, meeting for the first time in the fall of 1993.

The Task Force reviewed various resource materials but decided to design its own program in order to focus on the Canadian Anglican scene, not neglecting to incorporate anything found useful from other sources. Originally the plan called for parishes and other groups to go through the program and provide feedback to the Task Force by the end of 1994 so that an appropriate report might be made to General Synod the following June. However, as is often the case, delays were encountered and it wasn't until October 1994 that the Task Force issued its six-week Study Program entitled *Hearing Diverse Voices, Seeking Common Ground*, comprised mainly of a booklet and an accompanying video. Diocesan bishops were asked to make this available to parishes and other groups within the Church so that feedback could be sent to the Task Force by the end of April 1995.

(c) The Study: *Hearing Diverse Voices, Seeking Common Ground*

1) Introduction: A Narrow-Minded Question

The following analysis is an attempt to answer the single question: "Why is this Study Program deficient from a traditional/orthodox point of view?". The purpose is not merely to illustrate its failures but to zero in on how it impacts on that part of the Church which does not share the assumptions of those who put it together. What I have to say is not to be taken as implying there was no good at all in the Study. A fuller investigation would provide a more balanced picture but it would not, I believe, necessitate any serious revision of my basic contention that the Study is critically flawed in both process and content.

2) The Process: Going Our Way?

(A) Common Ground is Holy Ground

The basic problem here is revealed in the title of the study. In the past, when the Church was seeking guidance regarding any particular issue it went to the Scriptures and prayerfully examined them in the light of tradition and reason. This was because the Scriptures have been regarded as the Word of God and thus the way in which he has revealed himself and his will for humanity.

The assumption that seems to be guiding this Study, on the other hand, is that God's direction will be discovered by listening to one another as members of the Church and coming to some kind of consensus. The Church is elevated to the role of bearing the ongoing revelation while the Bible is relegated to being one of the resources which are called upon in the process. The Chairwoman of the Task Force expressed the hope that the Study would be used by many who would then "..add their voices to help discern 'the mind of the church.'" (p. 5) For her, and for many, it is the latter which seems to be of final importance. Such a view assumes that once we have achieved consensus we have arrived at the will of God.

(B) Church Over Scripture: A Great Leap Forward?

For those of traditional/orthodox persuasion this only means that we have a consensus. Although consensus is a worthy goal it is not to be confused with the will of God. The measure of truth lies first of all in the Bible. If it does not speak clearly then it is necessary, for the sake of institutional life, to seek consensus. In this case, again from the traditional/orthodox perspective, some of us have chosen to set aside the clear teaching of Scripture in favour of finding a consensus. This elevates the Church above Scripture and is a breathtaking departure from our tradition. The acceptance of such a process signals a significant moment in the development of our self-understanding as a Church and sets us on a course untried and undebated.

(C) No Debate Please, We're Inclusive

But debate is not on the agenda anymore. Today the word is "dialogue". This brings us to another objection to the process set out in this Study: its radical commitment to inclusivity. This is so thorough that it makes virtually impossible any serious interaction between persons with varying points of view. It is only permissible, apparently, to state one's position. These opinions are simply given to us as alternatives, but we are given no tools or means by which to assess them, to weigh them or to make any kind of judgment about them. This is especially evident in the chapters on Scripture, Ethics and Healing. The author of the first of these, the New Testament scholar Dr. Terry Donaldson, is quite explicit on this point. After an imaginative reading of Romans 1:26-7, in an attempt to listen to the voices of tradition and experience as a kind of dialogue, he says:

> I do not try to play the role of adjudicator, prescribing which voices should be given precedence, or which arguments should be given more weight than others. This is a task for the church as a whole, under the guidance of the Holy Spirit. (p. 41)

This is a strange statement to make in a study which is prescribed in order to assist "the whole church" to sort out this complex issue. We are effectively denied Dr. Donaldson's considered opinion regarding the only section of Scripture with which he does deal. Surely, as ordinary Anglicans we need his help and we also need to hear from other scholars in rebuttal so that we can weigh the relevant arguments. As it is we are left in thin air.

The same is true of the Study's subsequent chapter which looks at the other major Bible passages which refer to (or some have taken to refer to) homosexuality. The Study is clearly not designed so much as to help us to sort out the truth as to expose us to a variety of viewpoints, all of which are to be accepted and respected simply because they are held by bona fide members of the Church. While there are many excellent suggestions for small group discussion they include an attempt to avoid conflict by discouraging forms of "dialogue" which suggest someone is right or wrong (p. 12). The implication is that one has to accept all the points of view that exist in the Church as valid in order to be respectful and open to one another. Is it still necessary to point out that this is precisely the method of theological liberalism? It has no real way of making judging between one experience and another, so all are acceptable. Except one. That will come out clearly as we continue our look at this Study.

(D) It's Not a Multiple Choice Question

Those who prepared this study have already decided that it is improper even to suggest that the homosexual "lifestyle" is not Christian. We are told, for instance, that one of the purposes of the study is to "..elicit the wisdom of our church to enable it to make informed and responsible decisions *which will further include lesbian and gay people in the life of our community.*" (p. 6) In Session Five, under the title "Exploring Our Call to be One in Christ", we find the following purpose for that section:

> Despite the many different thoughts and feelings about homosexuality and homosexual relationships, lesbian and gay Christians are our sisters and brothers in Christ. We need to recognize those ways in which we exclude them from our community and *identify ways to become more inviting and inclusive.* (p. 75, my italics)

Now it would seem to many that the whole reason for the Study is to help us determine whether or not we should be more inclusive. It seems odd, to say the least, that this issue has already been decided by the authors of this study. In a truly open-ended study we would expect that, after the Church has had a chance to examine this issue thoroughly, the proper decision might be to support the status quo or even to exclude homosexuals more than we do already (not that I would at all support such a view). But these authors seem not to regard these options as possibilities at all. In fact they go out of their way to try to open the door further to homosexuals and homosexual relationships within the Church.

In their view, apparently, the fact that practicing homosexuals are in the Church means that their voice is authentically Christian. Of course their voice, and every voice, must be heard. But is it wise to present them as if they were all on a par with one another? The impression given is that all are to be accepted and that it is improper to pass judgement on any. This surely raises the question of the point of the exercise. The issue seems to be decided even before we start.

(E) Gaining Experience

One final point. Given the shape of the process already described, it is plain to see that it fits hand in glove with the liberal religion's agenda. We have already seen how liberals come to many of their convictions based on their own experience. If they experience Muslims as decent human beings they then conclude, against Scripture and tradition, that Muslims have no need of coming to Christ (see pp. 81-2). It is therefore only natural for them to think that the way to advance the cause of homosexuals is to have as many Church members as possible experience them in a positive light. While the

Study may not have been designed with this goal explicitly in view, the way it exposes participants to homosexuals and their views lends itself well to such a purpose. In this sense it is difficult to imagine a better tool for the advancement of liberal opinion.

(F) Conclusion: More Help Wanted

It is very difficult to escape the impression that this Study is designed to gain acceptance for the practicing homosexual, than to help us sort out the truth. It offers little to help the Church make the necessary *judgements* about the various opinions that are expressed. If all voices are to be heard and accepted as equally valid, on what possible basis could any be rejected? Thus the point of the exercise is not to weigh the various options but to accept the inclusivist assumptions so boldly stated by the designers of the Study. For many of us such an approach is woefully inadequate. We need more help than this. We could accept adulterers or child molesters on the same grounds of inclusion.

3) The Content: Disturbing Questions

The impression of bias gained through a look at the Study's *process* is powerfully reinforced when we examine its *substance*. The material in the chapters dealing with ethics and science are especially questionable.

(A) This Is Ethical?

As to the first of these, those Christians who, when deciding what to do in a particular situation, first ask "Is this action right, is it in accordance with the rules?", are characterized as having a "duty" ethic and following a God who is primarily an authoritative law-giver. When confronted with the question of homosexuality they "look for a Biblical command", as Tom Mabey, the author of this part of the Study (pp. 53-5) puts it. This is clearly a reference to traditional/orthodox ethics.

In contrast we are introduced to "interactive ethics" which asks, "Is this [course of action] responsible? Is it a constructive response to the relationships and environment?" This approach is what others have called "situational ethics" and is characteristic of what I have called the liberal position. Mabey tells us that in this system, "Actions reflect authentic meaning in relationships and contribute to ongoing development of mature relationships." God is viewed as an "interactor through ongoing covenants." In responding to homosexuality this approach seeks for "responsible and mature relationship" as the primary goal.

Besides missing altogether the essence of biblical ethics (as the dynamic expression of the new life of Christ in the believer under the direction of Scripture and the indwelling Holy Spirit, cf. J. I. Packer, *Keep In Step With the Spirit*, 1984, esp. pp. 108 ff.), the language that Mabey employs is self-evidently prejudicial. It is clearly designed to cast "duty" ethics in a bad light compared with the"constructive responses" called for by "interactive" ethics. This kind of presentation is only another way of excluding. Dr. Mabey's distortion of New Testament ethics and his less than subtle use of preferential language leave no doubt as to which system we should adopt. There is no real argument given for this superiority. It would have been much wiser to have a proponent of each ethical system make a vigorous presentation and allow us to weigh one against the other. Naturally this would require more work and time. Do we deserve less?

(B) This Is Scientific?

The predisposition towards the liberal view is even less subtle in the chapter entitled "What Science is Saying" (pp. 30-2). Here, at least, one would expect a fair and balanced outline of the scientific information available about homosexuality so that Anglicans might be able to base their decision on the facts. Instead, one finds a piece of work which seems more designed to obscure than to enlighten. When referring to the long-established evidence that homosexuality is related to certain patterns within their families, the author, Dr. Donald Meen, says, "...systematic study has shown no family characteristic which appears *only* in their families, and *never* in the families of heterosexuals." (my italics). Of course this is a true statement but it is irrelevant and extremely misleading. No scientific study could possibly provide this kind of absolute conclusion. In this area science can only provide us with patterns and probabilities. Dr. Meen seems to want to avoid any suggestion that environment has something to do with the formation of the homosexual.

This same "avoidance syndrome" is evident in his oblique reference to gay promiscuity: "It does appear that more gay couples choose to have relationships which are not sexually exclusive ("monogamous") than lesbian or heterosexual couples do." The fuller truth is that gay males are notoriously promiscuous, with one study showing, for example, that *83 per cent of them have had sexual relations with 50 or more partners in their lifetimes and that 28 per cent have had a thousand or more homosexual partners!* (quoted in *A Wholesome Example: Sexual Morality and the Episcopal Church*, Robert. W. Prichard, ed., 1992, p. 81-2) Surely the Church should be fully aware of these matters if it is going to open the door to any acceptance of homosexual practice. The rest of Dr. Meen's article gives scant attention to the wide variety of "scientific" debates that rage over this territory. Instead of letting us judge for ourselves he has plotted our route for us and its destination is clear. It comes as no surprise to learn that he himself is a homosexual gay-rights activist. Although the Church certainly needs to hear from Dr. Meen (and the other authors in this study), what they say needs to be set against a more balanced presentation so that we can wrestle with reality as much as possible in this very controversial and complex matter. We need to know what is at stake.

(C) Is This the Question?

Even the question we are being asked to answer has not been clearly articulated. Is the Church being asked simply to endorse homosexual practice itself or rather to endorse it only within the limits of a lifelong commitment to a monogamous relationship? If it is the latter then we would expect its advocates to be clearly and loudly asserting that homosexual relations outside such a "union" are just as unacceptable (i.e., sinful) as adultery. This would also mean, if the figures quoted above are close to the truth, that more than 83 per cent of male homosexuals would still be excluded by the Church. However, since there have been no such assertions and since the debate so far has focused on a blanket inclusivity (as in this Study), one is forced to assume that the Church is being asked to accept homosexual practice per se and this would include the acceptance of a level of promiscuity beyond the imagination of most members.

Such a move would entail the destruction of any serious idea of faithfulness in relationship to sexual activity. How could the Church insist on adultery as a sin that requires repentance and restoration when it condones homosexual promiscuity? It is worth noting that the road to acceptance of homosexuality in the United Church of Canada was paved by much talk of "loving and faithful relationships" but already at least one United Church congregation has proclaimed itself "a church that includes gays, lesbians, *bisexuals* and *transsexuals*" (my italics). With this development, obviously, any talk about "faithful monogamy" is irrelevant.

Will the homosexual lobby within the Church never be satisfied until there is full acceptance of all homosexual sexual activity? One gets the distinct impression that they are prepared to talk about faithful monogamous relationships only as an interim step toward that goal. Until we know precisely the implications of what we are being asked to approve, we had better proceed with extreme caution.

4) The Results: No End in Sight

Whatever its strengths and weaknesses, the Study was issued in the fall of 1994 and the Task Force was able to report to the 1995 General Synod that more than 2500 people had participated in the program. Not all dioceses took part in the program or were represented in the feedback. Many people, though, did submit responses and the Task Force "...worked to give focus to their voices." (General Synod 1995 Report, p. 9) A variety of viewpoints found expression just as they did the discussion which followed on the Synod floor. In response to all this the Synod:

> AGREED to affirm the presence and contributions of gay men and lesbians in the life of the church and to condemn bigotry, violence and hatred directed toward any due to their sexual orientation.
>
> AGREED to encourage parishes and dioceses to continue, deepen, extend and adapt the learning, reflection and dialogue identified by the Task Force on Homosexuality and Homosexual Relationships...to encourage parishes and dioceses to [ongoing dialogue on a number of issues identified by the Task Force] and to request the Faith, Worship and Ministry Committee [of General Synod] to make provision to ensure that this process continues at the parish and diocesan levels and that a report be made at the next General Synod.
>
> AGREED to request that the Primate continue to encourage dialogue on "homosexuality and homosexual relationships" throughout the church.
>
> AGREED to request the House of Bishops to indicate whether it is currently reviewing or intends to review its 1979 Statement and Guidelines on Human Sexuality. (General Synod 1995 Report, p. 9)

In passing these resolutions General Synod has expressed its continuing openness to changing the Church's teaching in this area. The next General Synod, in May of 1998, is clearly going to have this all back on its plate in some form or other. *Indeed, the last Synod tabled a resolution which called for "broad-based consultations within the Anglican Church of Canada concerning the liturgical recognition of committed monogamous same-gender unions".* (see Minutes of General Synod, p. 120).

The issue of same-sex unions, along with that of the ordination of practicing homosexuals, are the two main ways in which this whole question presents itself in the life of the Church. They are, of course, two sides of the same coin. If same-sex unions are blessed then what is to bar a person in such a relationship from ordination? Similarly, if someone who is a practicing homosexual is permitted to be ordained, presumably the relationship they are in is blessed by the Church. While the House of Bishops have recently re-affirmed their current intention not to move on these items, they did so in a way that strongly indicates an openness to change much like that expressed in the above resolutions. It was certainly not the drawing of a line in the sand (see "Behind the Purple Door, p. 149). In any event, great pressure will continue to bear on the next Synod and its successors to cross that line.

5) Conclusion: Give *Every* Voice a Voice

Given the lack of clarity surrounding this issue, the potential for serious division and the enormous implications for our whole system of sexual morality, it would seem to be of utmost importance that we proceed very carefully and thoroughly. While *Hearing Diverse Voices, Seeking Common Ground* can serve as a part of that process it fails to give adequate voice to the traditional/orthodox positions and arguments.

If the Church is truly serious about hearing all the voices then each must be invited to speak for itself in its own way. Every position, if it is truly to be respected and not merely patronized, deserves the right to put its best case forward. We must also find a way to honestly and respectfully *debate* these matters, not just present them in a "some say this, some say that" format.. How else can the membership of the Church possibly weigh the evidence, the arguments and the responses to those arguments? This is a very complex issue and it deserves our best effort. Much depends on it.

At the very least the Study Program should include, in the interest of fairness and balance, other mandatory reading which gives voice to other ways, other perspectives (I would strongly recommend *A Wholesome Example: Sexual Morality and the Episcopal Church*, Robert W. Prichard, ed., 1992). No doubt many will disagree with this assessment and insist that this Study is the only one we need. To you I simply say that is your voice and not mine. Nor that of many others in our Church. Please let *us* speak. If we feel excluded by this Study and by other actions of the National Church, take *our* word for it. That is what real listening is all about.

(iii) Remembrance of Things Past

It is impossible to grasp the import of these developments for the Church if we do not go back and remind ourselves of our overall situation. We have been so focussed on one particular tree (homosexuality) that we are in danger of losing sight of the forest (the crisis of two religions). Now is the time to step back and retrace our steps in order to see how we have gotten to this point in the argument. In so doing we will be better able to both assess the present situation and also get a better sense of what might lie ahead. What follows is a summary of what we have discovered so far.

1) From its beginning "catholic", or what I have called traditional/orthodox Christianity, has been built upon the assumption that the Bible is the very Word of God and is utterly truthful in what it teaches. The whole belief-structure of Christianity rises out of this fundamental conviction. It has guided doctrinal understanding and debate for two thousand years.

2) The Anglican Church, as part of the catholic and apostolic church, has both explicitly and implicitly agreed with this view of Scripture.

3) In the last century liberalism was introduced into the life of the Church. Starting from a rejection of the traditional view of the Bible it sought to adapt the teaching of the Church to the new theories of science and culture.

4) The basic principles of liberalism are inclusiveness, universalism and the authority of experience. These, along with liberalism's ever-changing faces, have proven to be incompatible with the traditional/orthodox faith upon which the Church was founded. It is, in fact, another religion altogether. As a result there are two religions in the same Church.

5) The denomination is in serious decline and faces crisis on many fronts.

6) Many of the problems in the Church, especially the decline in membership, are either the direct result of liberalism or have been worsened by its influence.

7) The unacknowledged clash between the two religions is the major factor in the gridlock that afflicts the denomination.

8) Both sides have found themselves backed into opposite corners over the secondary issue of homosexual practice. Each side rightly sees its fundamental principles at stake and is unprepared to back away from its position.

None of the developments at the national level are likely to lessen the extreme danger of the situation. On the one hand the official leadership of the

Church, both General Synod and the House of Bishops have continued to push for openness and dialogue on the homosexual question. This cannot satisfy the traditional/orthodox side. For them the Scripture is clear and there is no possibility of moving away from its teaching. On the other hand the Bishops have, at least for the time being, re-affirmed their ban on ordaining practicing homosexuals and the blessing of same-sex unions. This cannot satisfy the liberals. The pressure will continue to build. How much more can we take? What will happen if it blows?

CHAPTER SIX

Fault Prophecy

"You know how to interpret the earth and the sky. How is it that you don't know how to interpret this present time?" (Luke 12:56)

(i) Introduction: Into To the Abyss?

This chapter marks a significant turn in my argument. If the first five chapters can be referred to as the historical section, the next five fall into the prophetic category. As I admitted in the Introduction I am neither a prophet nor the son of a prophet. However, some things are obvious even to an amateur like me. Seeing two trains speeding toward each other on the same track enables you to make certain predictions with a high degree of confidence! That is, it is possible to see some distance into the future, at least, by carefully observing the past and the present in order to discern the direction events are taking. These can then be projected into the future. That is why we had to go through the first five chapters.

My basic and most important point is this: *given both its recent history and its current situation any further movement toward the acceptance of homosexual practice will force the Anglican Church of Canada into a divisive trauma so serious that it is difficult to see any happy resolution. A series of interconnected responses would be set in motion that could only end in a truly frightening plunge into the "abyss"* . I believe this conclusion to be unarguable. It is so obviously true that it almost goes without saying. Indeed there *is* a great silence about this, but for another reason altogether. It is just to hard a truth to face. But face it we must. This is the focus of what follows.

(ii) Finding Faults

In geology, a fault is defined as a fracturing in the earth's crust caused by massive forces at work beneath the surface. The most famous of these is the San Andreas Fault which runs roughly north and south through much of California. By studying these geological phenomena and the history of past earthquake activity in a particular area scientists are able to predict the pattern of destruction that would occur in the event of a major earthquake. The famous Richter Scale was developed to measure the intensity of these upheavals and the tremors which sometimes precede them.

Similarly it is possible to trace the fault lines of tension already present in the Anglican Church of Canada in order to predict what might happen if an "earthquake" were to hit. When we combine this with a consideration of the tremors that have already been felt we too can map out the future based on an ecclesiastical Richter Scale. This chapter will carefully trace the "fault lines" of unstable conditions that already exist just beneath the surface in the Church, taking into account recent events that could be seen as tremors warning of future trouble.

As any geologist will admit, however, it is impossible to predict the exact path of destruction because of the complexity of nature. Similarly it must not be assumed that what follows here is offered with a high degree of precision. Prophecy is always a tricky business. In spite of this, it is possible to predict the general *pattern* of destruction. If you have discovered a major fault and if it lies in a region subject to earthquake activity then you know roughly what is going to happen in the actual event. You would do your best to alert the population to the danger in the hope that they would make the appropriate preparations.

(iii) The Church's Fault Line

(a) Introduction: Living At the Epicentre

It is within the context of this "fault line" metaphor that we can better perceive the current reality facing the Anglican Church of Canada. It is, in fact, sitting on top of a major fault line running between two incompatible religions. Any official movement to affirm homosexual practice would serve as the trigger to set off a violent earthquake of reaction. The underlying division of the Church would be forced to the surface, tearing apart along the already discernible fault lines and opening up an infinite abyss.

My argument is based on the simple fact that there would be many Anglicans who would conclude that they could not in good conscience remain in a Church that has officially abandoned biblical religion and the catholic faith. They would leave. This would be bad enough for a denomination that has endured years of gradually shrinking numbers and income. This new exodus, however, would not be a quiet one, leaving in single file out the back door. Rather, it would be so noisy and so widespread that the resulting damage might seriously cripple the Church for the foreseeable future. It would not be pretty.

There are two possible scenarios. We might describe them as "Doing it Their Way" and "Doing It Our Way". The first of these refers to the fact that this possibility has already been played out in other denominations. It is always instructive to pay attention to how things have worked out in history. The second refers to how factors unique to the Anglican Church of Canada need to be taken into consideration. These will no doubt take us in our own peculiar direction.

One caution before we proceed: the image of earthquake cannot be pressed too far. When we think of an earthquake we inevitably think of sudden destruction. We can predict the prevailing path of such destruction once it is triggered. But at the same time it must be admitted that the *pace* of events is harder to predict. It may take quite a bit of time for all of these things to happen in the real life of the Church. On the other hand they may take place with dizzying speed. Personally I think matters will progress faster in our circumstances than they have in others. However, even if they move in slow motion the end result will be the same. And it still will not be pretty.

(b) Misery Loves Company: Doing It *Their* Way

1) Exhibit "A": The United Church of Canada

At the very least Anglicans should expect the same situation that unfolded (and continues to unfold) in the United Church of Canada. It is difficult to over-estimate the amount of pain and suffering which that denomination has endured since it went over the edge of the abyss several years ago. Congregations erupted in acrimony and a significant number decided to leave. Many found a ready home in the Congregational Church, giving it an unprecedented growth spurt. Families were split and long friendships destroyed.

Here in Eastern Canada the strife continues to this day. We have recently been treated to the spectacle of a local presbytery (diocese) disassociating itself from one of its ministers who had conducted a service of "covenanting" between two homosexuals. The minister's own congregation was split right down the middle and now, a year later, a beautiful stone church is up for sale. All of this was played out on the front page of the local newspaper. It is difficult for we Anglicans to imagine such open hostility and the pain, turmoil and stress it brings but we can be assured that this is precisely what will happen in our own Church in the wake of a decision to accept the practice of homosexuality. It *always* does. This is not only evidenced by the experience of the United Church but by that of a number of denominations in the United States. It seems to be a universal rule that wherever this issue is pressed serious division and strife are sure to follow. It is exceedingly unfortunate. It is a blow to the cause of Christ. But it is part of the reality that we must face.

2) Circles Within Circles

One of the seemingly inevitable aspects of these developments is the formation of a "church within the Church" as those faithful to the traditional/orthodox faith who do remain in the denomination try to come together for strength and encouragement. The United Church of Canada has the "Community of Concern" while the Episcopal Church has the "American Anglican Congress". Parishes associated with the Congress intend to advertise this fact on the sign outside the Church thus keeping the ugly division before the world. Furthermore, Episcopalians have just suffered through a heresy trial which saw one of their retired bishops acquitted because the court said that, while he had knowingly ordained a practicing homosexual, this was a matter of church discipline and not of doctrine. Since, in their opinion, the charge of heresy can only be applied in matters of doctrine, the bishop technically could not be guilty of "heresy". Whatever one thinks of these actions the fact remains that open and bitter conflict and division continue to plague those Churches which have officially or unofficially moved to accept homosexual practice. This is reason enough to pull back from the brink.

3) It Can't Happen To Us?

(A) Introduction: Getting a Sense of Things

For those who continue to believe that the Anglican Church of Canada may nevertheless be exempt from all or much of this we need only consider the recent history of the denomination. The trauma is *already* underway. While it may not be as visible as it is in other denominations, it is no less real. This should lead us to consider seriously the possibility of worse, much worse to come. At the very least it forces us to acknowledge that we would share in the same difficulties other Churches have encountered. We are not exempt. What we are seeing now are the early tremors of the "big one" yet to come. Let us then set up a few sensing devices and see what we can find.

(B) A Road Well-Travelled

As far as individuals are concerned, we have already examined the "culture of leaving" (see especially p. 93). For years people have been making the painful decision to leave the Anglican Church of Canada largely because they have perceived its drift away from the traditional/orthodox Christian faith. The key word here is "perceived". For a number of reasons, but mostly because many of them are deeply committed, articulate and aware of their Christian faith, these "leavers" were able to see what was really going on in the Church and, powerless to do anything about it, decided regretfully to move on to a denomination that kept the faith.

They have left as individuals or, perhaps more often, as families. Their leaving has blazed a trail of tears, making it easier for others to follow in the same direction, in the channel they have created. While they have not, in the past, been taking this step directly in response to the position of the Church on the specific question of homosexuality, many perhaps sensed an unwillingness of the Bishops, in their Statement of 1979 (see p. 117), to call the practice of homosexuality a sin and to demand repentance along with the commitment to celibacy. Some saw this, correctly, as it turns out, as the thin edge of the wedge and concluded that the Church was moving slowly but surely in a direction away from Biblical truth.

I personally remember talking with a former Layreader and his wife who had come to just this conclusion in the early 1980's and had made the painful decision to leave. I remember trying to explain the careful wording of the Statement to them and how I thought it upheld the Biblical position. They would have none of it. Today I feel they were more right than wrong, at least in their perception if not in their action. The Statement only deals with the matter in a formal way, asking homosexual priests only to conform to the outward appearances rather than insisting on heart and mind fully in agreement with the Biblical position. As a result it was legitimate to ordain homosexuals who were advocates of homosexual practice but who themselves agreed to abstain. There is strong anecdotal evidence to suggest that some broke this vow once they were ordained and suffered no disciplinary action as a result. Certainly there was little pastoral support put in place to help these men maintain a commitment that is notoriously difficult to keep even with the best of intentions. In these circumstances the Church was only asking for trouble.

Whatever the reasons, the departure of so many enthusiastic Christians from our Church has robbed it of much-needed vitality. Not only did they take their wallets with them (that was bad enough!) but also they took their many gifts of ministry, their keen interest in spiritual matters, their wisdom, their commitment to the mission of the Church, their willingness to shoulder much of the burden of parish activities, their knowledge of the Bible and its message and last but not least, their deep devotion to our Lord Jesus. Perhaps it is not going too far to suggest that their departure led to yet further losses to the Church as its overall vitality declined and many found it spiritually moribund. There is no doubt at all that losing these parishioners has caused grave harm to the Church. Many parish priests would give their right arm to have them back. I know this from personal experience. Saddest of all, at its official levels at least, the ACC does not seem to care.

(C) Reaching a Critical Mass

It is not only individuals that are already leaving. In the February 1996 edition of the Anglican Journal it was reported that virtually the entire congregation of the parish of St. Alban's, in Port Alberni, BC, had voted to leave the Anglican Church of Canada. The Primate dismissed this as an isolated event, suggesting that it only showed that "one parish ("...a small group of people from one part of the country...") is unhappy with the actions of General Synod". In fact, however, there are a number of reasons why this departure has very serious implications for us all.

For one thing there are many, many Anglicans from one coast to the other who find themselves in agreement with the published statements by the Rev. John Cox, rector of St. Alban's. It would be fair to say that almost all those attending the Essentials 94 conference in Montreal (over 700) would have little cause to argue with Mr. Cox's views as printed in the Anglican Journal. Add to them the combined total membership of the Prayer Book Society (traditionalist), Barnabas Ministries (evangelical) and Anglicans Renewal Ministries (charismatic) along with all those who are sympathetic to their positions and you have a considerable number of people and parishes indeed. The vast majority of them, however, while sharing Rev. Cox's perspective on the problems facing the Church, remain convinced that the best option for the present, at least, is to continue to work and pray for change from within.

What seems to have triggered the action taken in Port Alberni is a combination of intense frustration with the official structures of the Church and considerations unique to that particular parish. The details are sketchy in reference to the latter and in any event they would be both inappropriate and irrelevant to our discussion here. As to the former, I have already alluded to the strong sense of frustration and powerlessness that many Anglicans are experiencing. Here is how Mr. Cox has expressed this in reference to his own congregation:

> On the parish level we...have felt unsupported in our ministry and have been in the awkward position of having to explain statements by leaders that appear to many as being inconsistent with the Christian Gospel...It is

not, and should not, be our function to hold the leadership accountable to uphold traditional Christian values and teaching - indeed it should be the other way round!...*(i.e., it is the leadership which should be defending the faith on behalf of the faithful*-my comment*)*

The current direction of the Anglican Church has not encouraged or enriched local ministry and in fact has been a major factor draining energy and attention away from what we believe Jesus would have us focus on....

We believe that we have genuinely attempted to make a meaningful contribution to the life and ministry of the Anglican Church and we have repeatedly voiced concerns about [various] issues ...We have done so at deanery level, diocesan conferences, synods, and in personal conversations. We have been told that we have been heard but if feels more like a grudging toleration....

We are choosing to be pro-active in our identity as a church rather than waiting to see what will happen at the next Synod...and the next...*The Good News is too good and the mission of the Lord Jesus too great for us to wait in limbo any longer!* (his italics)

We are convinced that our efforts should be poured into reaching out into the world to share the Gospel with those who are lost, and to share in the ministry of healing and hope with the wounded and the poor. Unfortunately the Anglican umbrella has become more of a hindrance and a liability than an asset in the fulfillment of this vision. We have found ourselves having to make a choice between seeking to salvage a crumbling institution or going out into world in the name of Christ to serve Him as best we can according to His agenda not ours.

(All quotes taken from a from a Statement by the Rev. John Cox in January 1996 entitled "Concerns Relating to the Anglican Church of Canada")

It is clear that this intense feeling of frustration became an intolerable burden for this particular parish. For one thing the leadership wanted some assurances that the diocese would cease its liberal drifting so that they could in good faith ask parishioners to invest in an expanded facility. Why put more capital into a "crumbling institution"? Their requests that the diocese define the limits of Christian belief and practice fell on unresponsive ears. They came to the conclusion that the way the ACC went about its business was fundamentally flawed and that further association with it was actually a serious hindrance to their efforts to proclaim and live out the Gospel! The parish simply wanted to get on with the job and not be caught up in fruitless internal debates which, in its judgement, were going to result in official departures from Biblical religion no matter what it said or did.

Before moving along in this discussion it is important to make a few further observations about the situation that unfolded in Port Alberni. From all accounts this was not a typical struggling Anglican parish. It was very much alive and growing, attracting young people and even considering expanding its facilities to accommodate the needs of ministry in the parish. And now it is gone. Just like many of the individuals and families who left before them, it was their very enthusiasm for the Christian faith that led to their departure. It is also important to note the heartache and bitterness that this whole affair has engendered, especially at the local level. To leave under these conditions is a great tragedy, leaving behind an unsightly trail of wounded souls. There was, as always, sin on both sides. Such division is always messy. In his letter to the diocesan clergy announcing the departure of this congregation, Bishop Barry Jenks noted, perhaps with a sense of irony, that it was the Week of Prayer for Christian Unity.

(D) Standing Like Men, Essentially

While it would appear that other local factors have contributed to the level of frustration at St. Alban"s, it is also of great import for the whole Church that many Anglicans can identify with the dilemma faced by this congregation. They feel a similar type of frustration but it has not yet reached the same level. Perhaps typical of what is beginning to happen is the petition that a group called "Men of Essentials" has circulated:

> As members of the Anglican Church of Canada in the Diocese of British Columbia, we feel distraught and betrayed by the direction in which the leadership of the Church, both locally and nationally, appears to be going. We realize that many parish rectors have already spoken out on various issues of concern. Despite these actions, however, the views of the liberal element in the Church continue to exercise disproportionate influence in determining the direction of the Church. We feel that it is time for the 'lay people' of the Church to speak out...
>
> To voice clearly our dissatisfaction with the Church's new directions concerning homosexuality, the feminization of God, the loss of Trinitarian language, and the truth of the bodily resurrection of Jesus Christ...
>
> In making this appeal, we desire that the leadership of the Church not remain vague on these issues, that they refute statements credited to some Church leaders that are contrary to the Word of God ...

It is significant that this petition has arisen in the same diocese which saw the departure of most of the parish of Port Alberni. Indeed, the sentiments expressed are remarkably similar in both situations. How many parishes have a majority of members who feel the same way and how long will they continue to cling to the hope that it is possible to effect change from within?

(E) A Double-Minded Church

It is certain that the pressure continues to build as the trends away from traditional/orthodox Christianity continue and while those who resist them feel that they remain unheard. To them, the liberal establishment has not responded appropriately to concerns about changes in theology. In fact there is often no response at all, as was the case with input into the process of liturgical revision that led to the BAS. The powers that be ask for input and it is provided in good faith but it has no discernible impact on the end product. It is possible that the input is rejected for good and sufficient cause. It is also possible that it has been ignored. The point is that no discourse is generated, no debate is set in motion and no specific reasons are given for the exclusion of traditional/orthodox views. The two sides think so differently that they are unable to communicate with one another.

Part of this seems to be because liberals honestly do not comprehend how seriously those in the traditional/orthodox camp take these departures from our official positions. Having a different understanding of the function of symbol and language, liberals really feel that they are not making any departures at all. In their view, they are simply articulating the faith in ways appropriate to their culture like Christians have always done. For liberals it is merely a matter of formulating a contemporary expression of the "unchanging faith".

Traditional/orthodox people, on the other hand, find it impossible to make a distinction between the faith and its original expression in the Scriptures. This is not to deny that the Gospel is adapt itself to various cultures. But its basic shape and fundamental truths cannot be changed. There is no inarticulate "unchanging faith" which can somehow be separated from its expression. They see this idea as a modern construct which has no warrant in Scripture, reason or tradition as they understand them.

For the liberal it is perfectly consistent to say that the new language referring to God as "mother", for example, involves no change in faith while for anyone who is of traditional/orthodox persuasion the opposite is self-evident. Between these views there is no common ground. Again we are faced with the reality that we have two different and incompatible religions within the same denomination. It is my hope that what has been said in this book might contribute to an understanding of this situation and that further discussions will lead us closer to a resolution of our current gridlock.

(F) Conclusion: It *Is* Happening to Us!

We have every reason to expect that the Anglican Church of Canada will prove no exception to the rule. Forces presently at work within the institution guarantee that it will follow the same destructive path other denominations have taken if it affirms the practice of homosexuality. It will have passed the point of no return for many of its members, resulting in the exodus of significant numbers of individuals and even congregations. The fault lines already lie close to the surface. Even amateurs can tell which way it is going to go.

(c) The Diocese Factor: Doing It *Our* Way

1) Introduction: What a Difference a Diocese (Or Three) Makes

So far we have been treating the unfolding possibilities within the Anglican Church of Canada as parallel to the experience of other mainline denominations caught up in the same struggle. Without denying that Anglicans can expect to face a similar situation, there is a factor to consider which is perhaps unique to the Anglican Church of Canada. Its presence will have a very strong influence on the direction that events will take if movement is made toward the acceptance of the practice of homosexuality.

I refer here to the fact that there are three entire dioceses in Canada which have publicly gone on record with exceptionally strong stands opposed to any such development. It is impossible to overstate the significance of this fact for the debate which is now taking place in the Church as a whole. The dioceses in question are The Arctic, Fredericton and Yukon, each of which has taken a slightly different approach while clearly sharing common convictions.

2) Standing In the Ice: The Arctic

In the Diocese of the Arctic this has taken the form of a "Protocol on Sexual Misconduct" and in diocesan policy regarding qualifications for ministry. The following was passed as part of a motion regarding "Order and Eligibility for Licensing" at their 1996 synod:

> No person shall be eligible to hold license to minister in the Diocese of the Arctic who, while licensed or seeking license, ...willingly engages in homosexual, lesbian or bisexual practices.

3) Standing In the Mountains: Yukon

The Diocese of Yukon took the matter a step further and actually encoded an almost identically worded clause in their "licensing" canon (church law), Canon IV 26 (3) (A). Like the Arctic's approach, this canon also deals with a number of sexually related issues, not just homosexuality. The fact that this diocese has set this provision into its canon law is a clear indication of the depth of its conviction that homosexual practice is completely incompatible with the exercise of Christian ministry. The North is standing very firm on this issue.

4) Standing In the Trees: Fredericton

The Diocese of Fredericton, which takes in the entire province of New Brunswick, has taken a different route to the same destination. In June 1993 the diocesan Synod overwhelmingly endorsed the following motion:

> That this Synod affirm the clear Biblical and universally held teaching of the Church that sexual relationships between persons of the same sex are contrary to God's purpose and are thus sinful and that this affirmation be conveyed as a Memorial to General Synod.

Clearly this is more of a general rejection of homosexual practice than expressed by Yukon and the Arctic. While the latter dioceses concentrate on the qualifications for licensed ministry, Fredericton goes to the heart of the matter and articulates the reasons why many Anglicans (including, no doubt, those in the Arctic and Yukon) feel the way they do on this issue. To send this as a Memorial to General Synod is one way that a diocesan synod can communicate with the national synod. It is similar to sending a memo and is printed up in the convening circular which all General Synod delegates receive prior to gathering. Like any memo, it may or may not get noticed! It is worth noting that backroom liberal reluctance had a great deal to do with keeping this memorial off the floor of the last General Synod, as one of the key participants publicly acknowledged.

5) Standing In the Field?: Brandon

It is interesting also that in 1996 the diocese of Brandon asked the General Synod "...to proceed cautiously and give strong ear..." to that section of *The Montreal Declaration of Anglican Essentials* which reads in part:

> Adultery, fornication, and homosexual unions are intimacies contrary to God's design...Homophobia and all forms of sexual hypocrisy and abuse

> are evils against which Christians must ever be on their guard. The church may not lower God's standards for any of its members, but must honour God by upholding these standards tenaciously in face of society's departure from them.

While this motion was supported two to one by the laity, it is telling that it passed in the House of Clergy by only one vote. Again we see the familiar division between the pew and the pulpit that plagues our Church. We also see which side is more under the influence of liberalism.

6) Conclusion: A Cause for Pause

The bold actions taken by these dioceses should give the rest of the Church a further reason to consider carefully indeed what action it will take on this issue. It is critical to recognize that these dioceses have staked out their positions in the context of the contemporary debate. They represent current attitudes and cannot be seen as mere leftovers from a previous age. Some leaders see these actions as premature because the process devised by the National Church was not followed. On the other hand, it is possible to regard that process to be seriously compromised by its decidedly liberal bias. Besides, some Anglicans still regard the truth as given and not subject to modification through *any* process. This attitude appears to predominate in these four dioceses at least (if Brandon is included). From this perspective it may have seemed imperative to speak out in advance on an issue of such critical importance.

(iv) Fault Movements: Paths of Destruction

(a) Introduction: Trigger Points

Having examined the definite stands taken against the practice of homosexuality by at least three Canadian dioceses, we are in a better position to predict what will happen in the event of any contrary movement taking place in the Church. It will soon become obvious that because of these unique circumstances things will not unfold like they did in other denominations. The fault lines are just not the same and therefore the devastation resulting from an "earthquake" in the Anglican Church of Canada will take its own peculiar course. Even that will vary depending on where exactly the quake begins.

Therefore we must first ask ourselves from what part of the Church movement toward the acceptance of homosexual practice could come. In following the fault lines out from these "trigger points" we could then see what is likely to happen. Fortunately for us there are really only two ways in which this movement could begin. We will now take a look at each of these as a theoretical possibility. The next chapter will discuss the likelihood of either actually happening.

1) It's the Bishop's Fault

(A) Introduction: Breaking Ranks

First of all it is entirely possible that a liberal diocesan bishop will finally lose patience with the National Church and break ranks. Several of the bishops are adamant in their determination to have the Church change its mind and accept the practice of homosexuality. Moving in the context of his own diocese a bishop could press toward openly ordaining a practicing homosexual and authorizing the blessing of same-sex unions. And there are some dioceses which might go along.

Since a bishop and his diocese form the basic unit of the Church this is a perfectly legitimate (if impolitic) course of action and there is little that the Primate or anybody else could do about it, at least in the short run. This is exactly what has already taken place in the Episcopal Church south of the border.

(B) Trouble At Home: Parish Responses

In Canada there is little doubt that in whatever diocese this happens there will be a significant number of rectors and parishes who will find themselves seriously alienated from their bishop. While it is very difficult to predict what action they might take, it is certain that they will not remain idle. It is critical to grasp this point.

These parishes will regard their bishop to be endorsing sin and failing in his role as defender of the faith. Some may merely inform their bishop of their extreme unhappiness with the action he has taken. It is difficult to see how they could possibly accept episcopal ministry from their diocesan bishop in such circumstances and as a result they may request that they be provided with the services of an "orthodox" bishop. An official precedent for this has been set in England in connection with the issue of the ordination of women. Those parishes opposed to this development who find themselves with a bishop who is in fact ordaining women are permitted to have the services of another bishop. In the (American) Episcopal Church, where there is no such system in place, at least one parish apparently has posted armed guards at the door to keep their diocesan bishop out! (from the Internet, Episcopal Synod of America, Bulletin, October 23, 1997)

Others may take the further step of refusing to contribute some or all of their "fair share" to the diocesan budget. This may come about more at the instigation of lay people at annual meetings than it will from rectors. How the bishop and diocese would react to this is hard to say. Does the deliberate non-payment of diocesan apportionment constitute grounds for a bishop to dismiss the current parish vestry, wardens, synod delegates and rector? Undoubtedly such a move would be challenged in ecclesiastical court.

Finally, there will no doubt be some parishes who, like the parish of St. Alban's in Port Alberni, B.C., will vote to leave their diocese altogether. A number of these might even band together in this action and declare themselves the true successor to the official diocese. They could elect their own bishop and challenge in court the validity of the "other" bishop and any move he might make to deprive them of their property (which in the Anglican system is actually owned by the bishop). Whatever actions dissident parishes might take, they would certainly offer shelter to individual Anglicans who were leaving area parishes who opted to remain under the original bishop.

(C) Trouble At the Office: Diocesan Responses

Now add to this chaotic scene the fact that three or four entire *dioceses* have strongly affirmed the traditional/orthodox view of homosexuality. It is unlikely that they will simply ignore the plight of parishes who share the same theological perspective. These dioceses would have to ask themselves the same kinds of questions already faced by the dissenting parishes. They would be faced with making a very uncomfortable choice. They will have to support either the official structures and those in them (with whom they profoundly differ) or those at odds with those structures (and who share the same faith as their own).

This is not primarily about homosexuality. It is about two different and incompatible religions trying to share the same institution. There can be little doubt that the dioceses of Yukon, the Arctic and Fredericton (at least) would find a way to express their solidarity with their co-religionists in other dioceses. This linkage ensures that any liberal bishop who puts some of his parishes in an untenable position will have put the three dioceses in the same dilemma. How could they ignore the fact that those with whom they are in fundamental agreement are being pushed aside or even out of the same denomination? Something will have to give.

At the very least we could expect these dioceses to come to the public defense of the protesting parishes by issuing proclamations of sympathy and solidarity. They might also take the next logical step of declaring their own alienation from the bishop who had initiated the matter, perhaps to the point of declaring themselves out of communion with him. This is precisely what the dissenting parishes themselves did but in the case of dioceses taking similar action the ante is upped considerably.

For one thing we would have one basic unit of the Church (a diocese) taking on another. This is significant because parishes by themselves are at a distinct disadvantage in any struggle with their diocese. To have another bishop and diocese go to bat for you would make a considerable difference.

For another, such a move might precipitate schism in the Anglican Church of Canada. Many would feel very strongly that it is not these alienated parishes which should leave but rather the bishop (and the rest of his diocese) who has openly departed from the faith. The three dioceses would be sorely tempted to offer episcopal oversight to the parishes on the outs with their bishop rather than see them languish in ecclesiastical limbo or be lost forever to the Anglican Church. Such parishes could "join" a distant diocese that was committed to traditional/orthodox faith.

This would certainly stretch our understanding of a diocese as a geographical area under one bishop. However, the idea of a non-geographic diocese is already being explored by the National Church as it contemplates the possibility of setting up a single diocese for aboriginal Anglicans throughout Canada. This would be somewhat parallel to the Bishop Ordinary to the Canadian Forces who oversees Anglicans in uniform wherever they are in the world. The United States has already seen the development of the Episcopal Synod of America which has set itself up as a non-geographical synod for conservative parishes still in the Episcopal Church. Fantastic as all this may seem it is a reality which Canadian Anglicans need to keep in mind.

There remains one more radical (and less likely?) possibility to consider: dissenting parishes in a diocese that had "departed from the faith" might go so far as to elect their own "continuing" bishop. In turn, it might be that the bishops of Yukon, the Arctic and Fredericton, for example, involve themselves in his consecration and recognize him as the "true" bishop of the wayward diocese. And that, tragically, would be schism, pure and simple!

2) It's General Synod's Fault

(A) Introduction: Another Way to Go

The other way in which the Church could move toward the acceptance of homosexual practice would be through an act of General Synod. In this case, instead of a single bishop going his own way, a majority of delegates from across the whole country would make the decision. This too would result in serious conflict as the same three (or more) dioceses face not just a wayward bishop but a wayward National Church! As a result this fault line runs a significantly different course.

(B) Pushed To the Edge

At the very least the same three dioceses will refuse to ordain practicing homosexuals or bless same-sex unions. It must be emphasized that they will not see this as merely an in-house difference on a relatively unimportant issue. Rather, they will view the rest of the Church as having endorsed sin through a deliberate departure from the biblical faith of our tradition. This is much more problematic than a matter of order (women's ordination) or practice (divorce and remarriage) on which there were a range of legitimate interpretations of Scripture.

How long would it be, then, before these dioceses felt it necessary to take more drastic action to distance themselves from the actions of General Synod? Even if the issue were confined to this one difference of "opinion", the situation would be serious enough. But, as we have seen, there is every reason to think that the positions taken by the three dioceses on the question of homosexuality represent serious opposition to the general drift away from the traditional/orthodox positions of the Church. In other words, the same forces which have led to many individuals and parishes finding themselves in a state of extreme tension with the National Church are dominant in these dioceses. This makes it much more unlikely that drastic action could be avoided.

(C) Pushed Together

The dioceses of Yukon and the Arctic are financially dependent on the National Church and so would find it extremely costly to pull out of General Synod. However, if they did so or declared their desire to do so, there would be enormous psychological pressure on the diocese of Fredericton to take similar action and to withhold the almost $400,000 it now sends to Toronto, sending it instead to the two northern dioceses. How could it stand idly by and see these missionary dioceses suffer greatly for taking such principled action when it is in full agreement with their theological position? At the same time it would prove difficult to continue financial support of a National Church that had so clearly departed from biblical faith.

Is it even possible that the three dioceses in question will eventually declare themselves to be the true successors to the Anglican Church of Canada and disassociate themselves entirely from the other twenty-seven dioceses (assuming, of course, that they are not joined by a few others)? Where would this leave the individuals, congregations and those diocesan bishops who shared the position of the three dioceses but who merely by reason of geography remained in the "official" Church? What would happen to bishops, for example, if they find themselves in a diocese that is pushing them to ordain practicing homosexuals or in which some of the clergy are agitating to be able to bless same sex unions just as their colleagues in other dioceses are permitted to do? Would congregations seeking to leave the "official" Church seek episcopal oversight from the one of the three "continuing" diocesans? Certainly a number of these would be happy to divert their diocesan apportionment to the two northern dioceses. This might even have the happy effect of solving the chronic financial problems of the North and then some!

(D) A Shoving Match at Lambeth?

Beyond all this is the question of what will happen when the three bona fide diocesan bishops present themselves at the Lambeth Conference, the world gathering of Anglican bishops, especially if they do so declaring themselves to be the representatives of the true continuing Anglican Church of Canada. Will it be possible for the "official" National Church to declare that all the people of the diocese of Fredericton along with their bishop are no longer members of the Anglican Communion? Or vice-versa? Will Lambeth be able to tolerate two claims to legitimacy? This would be especially difficult to do when it would be the National Church itself which had clearly departed from the tradition still held by the vast majority within the Communion.

Thus a schism that involves entire dioceses could well precipitate a serious crisis in the world-wide Anglican Communion. The same choices that face the lower levels of the Church would have to be confronted at the higher while a means of defining Anglicanism and its limits would have to be devised. The great struggle of the two religions in the whole of the Communion would then come to a head. At the very least there is little doubt that this would constitute a serious challenge to the traditional approach of recognizing only institutional continuity. Suggesting that theological and spiritual continuity is of greater importance might set in motion a series of events that could radically alter the way the Communion sees itself. Perhaps at some point continuing Anglican bodies may be invited back into the fold! It might also open the door wider to the renewal of worldwide Anglicanism as it begins to ask the questions that should have been addressed several generations ago.

(v) Reality Checks: We Are Not Alone

Admittedly this all sounds rather fantastic. No wonder there is so little serious discussion of such matters in print. They are truly scary. But they are nevertheless very real possibilities. That this is so can be seen when we examine a couple of recent developments at the level of the worldwide Anglican Communion. Even more is actually taking place but these alone should shake us out of our complacency.

(a) The South is Rising: The Kuala Lumpur Statement

In February 1997 eighty delegates from dioceses and provinces in Africa, Asia, Latin America and Oceania met for the Second Anglican Encounter in the South in Kuala Lumpur, Malaysia. As such they represented millions of Anglicans in the expanding part of the Communion. With an eye on the upcoming Lambeth Conference in 1998, they addressed the issue of human sexuality from their perspective in the Third World. It is clear that they intend to meet the challenge of the liberalizing West head on. They issued a call to the rest of the Church to work together in order "...to reach a common mind before embarking on radical changes to Church discipline and moral teaching" (Article 11) and, in a powerful *Statement on Sexuality*, proclaimed the following:

> We are deeply concerned that the setting aside of biblical teaching in such actions as the ordination of practising homosexuals and the blessing of same-sex unions calls into question the authority of the Holy Scriptures. This is totally unacceptable to us. (Article 10)

Besides being a bold articulation of their position this Statement agrees with my point that it is the authority of Scripture which is truly at stake in the question of homosexuality.

But it does not end there. Worldwide support for the Kuala Lumpur Statement seems to be gathering momentum. For example, the Standing Committee of the Province of South East Asia overwhelmingly passed a motion adopting and endorsing the Statement. Not content with just doing that, it went on to take the position that "This Province support and be in communion with that part of the Anglican Communion which accepts and endorses the principles aforesaid and not otherwise." (For this and quotations above see the September 1997 edition of *The Prayer Book Society of Canada Newsletter*) This is pretty strong talk. It is reality.

(b) A Preliminary Bout: Spong vs. Carey

Also reality is a nasty confrontation between Bishop John Spong of the Episcopal diocese of Newark and Dr. George Carey, the Archbishop of Canterbury. Spong, who is the point-man for the liberal view of homosexual relations has recently written to all the Primates in the Anglican Communion accusing them, according to the London Daily Telegraph, "...of acting out of prejudice, fear and ignorance in their teaching". This seems to arise out of the rising worldwide support for the Kuala Lumpur Statement. In response, Dr. Carey published an open letter, saying "I am saddened by the hectoring and intemperate tone of your statement which appears to leave little room for the dialogue you demand."

The Archbishop goes on to point out that bishops from all over the Communion were getting behind the Kuala Lumpur document. He told Bishop Spong:

> I draw your attention to these facts because I want to be sure that everyone fully realizes the divisive potential of this, not just for the Communion but for people more generally. If bishops come to Lambeth (in July, 1988) wanting a showdown on this issue, I am quite clear that there will follow a very negative and destructive conflict...

Clearly there is a rumbling and a shaking coming on this issue that will indeed impact on the whole of the Anglican Communion. It may split it wide open. You don't have to take just my word for it. This is an urgent and serious matter.(Quotations from the Internet, Episcopal Synod of America Bulletin, November 27, 1997)

(vi) Conclusion: It's the Big One!

I trust that enough has been said to demonstrate that my own ruminations are not merely idle speculation. They have in fact been based on a careful reading of the fault lines that are already present and visible to those are willing to look. Once again I do not maintain that the details will work themselves out exactly as portrayed. No seismologist, ecclesiastical or otherwise, would make any such claim. However, the course of events undoubtedly will follow something of this general pattern. It is difficult to see how they could not, given the realities of the situation both in the Anglican Church of Canada and in the Anglican Communion at the present time. But the actual eruption, like all real earthquakes, will not be bound by our charts and maps, our neatly assembled facts and figures. It will go its own destructive way and no human being can stay its course.

CHAPTER SEVEN

Can These Bones Live?

The hand of the Lord was upon me, and he brought me out by the Spirit of the LORD and set me in the middle of a valley; it was full of bones. He led me back and forth among them, and I saw a great many bones on the floor of the valley, bones that were very dry. He asked me, "Son of man, can these bones live?
I said, "O Sovereign LORD, you alone know."
Then he said to me, "Prophecy to these bones and say to them, 'Dry bones, hear the word of the LORD!...I will make breath enter you, and you will come to life.' " (Ezekiel 37: 1-5)

(i) Introduction: A Pound of Prevention

The violent, spontaneous and unbridled ripping apart of the Church depicted in the last chapter would clearly be in no one's interest. In any such scenario it is finally impossible to tell how far the fault lines extend and how many new fissures would open up, greatly complicating an already perplexing picture. There can be little doubt that the human cost would be enormous. The anger and passion let loose would inevitably leave behind an ugly wake of damaged souls, broken relationships and bitter spirits. Surely none of this would be edifying to Christ and his church or would commend itself to the watching world. The entire resources of the denomination would be tied up for years in the struggle. This comes at a time when those resources are already spread very thinly indeed. There is little question that the energy spent in the conflict would at the least seriously weaken its present moribund condition.

Those pushing the homosexual agenda forward need to come to terms with the reality of the situation. The liberal side should ponder long and hard before it presses ahead with this issue in the current context. To the extent that they too wish to maintain order and good government they have, oddly enough, good reason to back away from the edge themselves. No one wishes to be responsible for schism. The potential harm that would come to the Church should be enough of a motive to wait until a better approach is developed. From the liberal point of view the temporary continuing injustice of not affirming homosexual practice must be weighed against the virtual destruction of the Anglican Church of Canada and all that means to thousands of faithful members.

Part of my purpose in writing at the present time is to help *prevent* all this from taking place. As an ecclesiastical seismologist I have been reading my charts and watching my gauges. I have even been on the scene a few times and felt the tremors myself. I know what is coming and I cannot remain silent. I love the Church and I so I raise my voice in warning. If the Church can be made to realize the danger that it is in, that the abyss is just ahead, then there is hope. Only then will it take the action necessary not only to avoid going over the edge but also to start out on the long road to recovery. I believe the possibilities for this are actually quite real. Let me explain.

(ii) A Pretty Big "If"

We need to begin by reminding ourselves all of the trauma I have predicted will only take place *if* a Bishop (and diocese) breaks ranks and permits the blessing of same-sex unions and/or ordains a practicing homosexual or *if* the National Synod decides to endorse the practice of homosexuality directly or indirectly. The question then becomes: "What is the likelihood that any of these trigger events will happen?"

At the present time there is no clear answer to this question. If we look at the past we can see that there has been considerable movement towards the acceptance of homosexual practice among some in the denomination. As a Church we have moved from being solidly against to being of two minds. The direction in which we are moving is clear. Certainly we are not becoming more convinced of the traditional position! This is not to say that those holding to the latter are changing their minds. They are dug in for good just like the dioceses of the Arctic, Yukon and Fredericton. Rather, those in the middle have been slowly warming to the liberal side and this, combined with Anglican reluctance to say "No!", has contributed to the sense of tension as the cord holding us all together gets stretched further and further. If nothing happens to stop this drifting then it will only be a question of "When?" instead of a question of "If".

Many Anglicans are aware that the House of Bishops recently issued a Statement on the issue of homosexuality. Some may even feel that it puts the matter to rest. It certainly is an important development, perhaps even a critical one. It deserves our close attention.

(iii) A House Divided: Where the Bishops Are

(a) Background: Behind the Purple Door

Meeting in April 1997, the House of Bishops "tested its current position" in regard to the 1979 Guidelines in reference to the ordination of homosexuals. It will be recalled from the discussion of the Guidelines in Chapter Five (p. 117) that these upheld the traditional/orthodox view that excluded practicing homosexuals from ordination. But "guidelines" are not the law and these settled very little. The bishops have been studying and reviewing them behind closed doors since 1991. After their April 1997 meeting they issued a Statement, for the first time going public with where they are. The results are quite interesting. They certainly show a House divided!

Out of the thirty-four bishops present (Canada has thirty dioceses, several of which have more than one bishop):

1. Ten members wished to retain the 1979 Guidelines in their present form;

2. Eighteen members wished to retain the original intention of the Guidelines, but update them in the light of new pastoral awareness.

3. Six members wished to retain the Guidelines in force while a task force worked on new guidelines.

The Statement then went on to say that the "House of Bishops thereby commits itself to retaining the 1979 Guidelines in principle, but intends to express them in a wider context of theological understanding and pastoral sensitivity...".(The New Brunswick Anglican, June 1997, p. 1)

It is obvious that the bishops were unable to come to a common mind. Those in the first group are clearly opposed to the ordination of practicing homosexuals. The third group, we can safely assume takes the opposite view. Of those in the middle there is little that can be concluded from this beyond what appears to be a willingness to soften the 1979 Guidelines. For example, in the accompanying survey of the bishops, twenty-three said the Church should be "more accepting and affirming of models of families other than the nuclear family" (New Brunswick Anglican, June 1997, p. 1). This could mean anything from single-parent families to "group marriages" to "living together" arrangements.

The bishops met again in October 1997 and issued their revision of the 1979 Guidelines as promised. After outlining the background it begins with the unqualified statement that "As Christians we believe that homosexual persons are created in the image and likeness of God...". This, like much of the Statement, could be taken in a number of ways. It goes on to affirm "...that all persons are brothers and sisters for whom Christ died." It is on the basis of these "theological insights" that the bishops support the equal protection for gay and lesbian persons under the law of the land. Many in the Church will regard these insights as extremely ambiguous and possibly misleading. From this point of view they constitute an inadequate basis for Church decisions. (See "To Universalism and Beyond" p. 73ff.)

While the bishops affirm that Holy Matrimony is confined to the union of male and female they do not rule out the possibility of accepting homosexual unions under another name than marriage.

> We continue to believe that committed same sex relationships should not be confused with Holy Matrimony. The house will not authorize any act that appears to promote this confusion. There is, and needs to be, ongoing discussion about how to respond appropriately to faithful and committed same sex relationships...
>
> We are not ready to authorize the blessing of relationships between persons of the same sex. However, in interpreting the Gospel, we must always reflect on the context to which it is addressed. We are, therefore, committed to ongoing study of human sexuality and of the nature and characteristics of human intimacy and family life as it exists in our society.

On the issue of the ordination of homosexual persons the Statement reaffirms that "...sexual orientation in and of itself is not a barrier to ordination or the practice of ministry within the church." What must be considered is the manner in which our sexuality is expressed.

> At ordination, candidates promise to live their lives and shape their relationships so as to provide a "wholesome example" to the people of God (BCP, p. 642). Exemplary behaviour for persons who are not married includes a commitment to remain chaste.

The bishops are clearly not prepared to bless same sex unions, at least for the time being. They remain divided over "...whether such relationships can be expressions of God's will and purpose". Calling for further study and dialogue they are open to the possibility of changing their minds. Until they do, if they do, they will continue to hold all unmarried ordination candidates to chastity.

(b) Here Today, Gone Tomorrow?

At best this most recent Statement can only be considered as a snapshot of where the bishops now are as a group. Much in it suggests that it is not to be taken as a final resting place. Phrased with studied ambiguity it remains open to movement toward acceptance of practicing homosexuality in the context of committed relationships. In this sense it gives some indication of the direction the House can be expected to go in the future.

Interestingly, Bishop Ingham of Vancouver agrees. In a recent interview he said that he will

> ...say to gays and lesbians in my diocese that the Statement can be interpreted hopefully, that the Church is moving. But it is not moving fast enough or far enough for those people who are, in part, excommunicated.
>
> There is no doubt which way this is going. The question is how long will it take? Canadian society is becoming much more accepting of gays and lesbians. The courts, the direction of civil law is toward equal rights. The Church seems to be lagging behind society. (both quotes from the Internet, Episcopal Synod of America Newsbrief, Pt.V, Nov. 14, 1997)

It is also critical to note that the bishops also defeated a motion to authorize what some are calling "the local option". Some of the bishops wanted approval to go it alone, to not wait for the rest of the Church before proceeding toward the acceptance of homosexual practice. This was an important decision for the House to make because, as we have seen ("It's the Bishop's Fault", p. 140ff.), exercising the local option would serve to set off an "earthquake" within the denomination. The very fact that such a motion was proposed indicates the readiness of some bishops to move on this issue. The fact that it was defeated may or may not prevent them from doing what they feel is the right thing. But it will probably delay any such action.

Those hoping for a strong bulwark against movement toward the acceptance of homosexual practice will no doubt find scant comfort in these most recent developments. But there is also reason to be grateful.

(c) Thank God for the Bishops!

The bishops, although not making any definitive stand, have given the Church a precious gift: time. What they have done is ensure the status quo for the near future. It is difficult to see how they could reverse themselves soon without losing all credibility. Their decision on the local option should at least slow down those bishops eager push ahead on the homosexuality issue in their own dioceses. Finally, any initiatives in this same direction which might come out of General Synod are going to have to take the Statement into account. If the House of Bishops is not ready to move, the Synod will not be ready either.

(d) Conclusion: A Holding Pattern

This adds up to the tentative conclusion that, *as long as this situation holds*, the Anglican Church of Canada should be spared the trauma of open schism, of going into the abyss. True, it shows every indication of being only a temporary respite but it *is* a respite. One would hope that it will last at least through the General Synod scheduled for May, 1998.

We must not, we dare not, squander the gift.

(iv) Redeeming the Time

(a) Introduction: A Golden Opportunity

We must begin with the realization that nothing has fundamentally changed. We still face all the horrors of the abyss. It is just that we can be reasonably assured that it should not open up for a while yet. But for any hope in the longer run the deeper issue that is driving us to the brink must be resolved. What may surprise us is that the circumstances we now face offer us an exciting and unprecedented opportunity to do just that.

We must allow this ugly confrontation over homosexuality to shake us loose of our unwillingness to deal with reality. It is time to end the denial. It is time to face the facts. There is just no way out of our mess until we open our collective eyes and see it for what it is. This is the necessary first step toward recovery and, difficult as it may be, we must take it. For it is also a step back from the abyss.

And the real issue is not homosexuality. There can be no question that it is an important issue in and of itself and needs to be sensitively resolved by every Christian community. But, and this is my main point, this cannot be done in the Anglican Church of Canada while we continue to come at the question with radically different theological principles. Our deep differences over homosexuality are the reflection of the fact that we are divided into two incompatible religions. This is what lies behind the overall crisis in our denomination. This is the real issue. We simply cannot come to a common mind on the homosexual question until we agree to some basic truths which can guide our discussion and our prayer.

(b) Three Giant Steps for General Synod

How can all this be translated into a program that will have any hope for success? Three things must happen. They all have to do with the upcoming General Synod in May 1998 at Montreal.

1) Support the Bishops' Stand

First of all the recent action of the bishops must be supported. Their decision to continue the ban on the blessing of same-sex unions and the ordination of practicing homosexuals has bought us valuable time by keeping the abyss at bay. But it is a fragile peace at best. The bishops themselves remain divided and have expressed themselves in such a way as to suggest they are willing to move away from their current position. Will what they have done be enough to discourage General Synod from taking a step itself toward accepting homosexual practice? Or will strong support from the floor for such action cause the bishops themselves to reconsider? It would be much better for the Church if General Synod members come prepared to support the bishops. This would guarantee, as much as anything could guarantee, that we will be granted enough time to get the task done.

2) Focus On the Real Crisis

Secondly, General Synod must focus itself on the crisis at hand. It must not, it cannot allow itself a "business as usual" attitude. To have another Synod which once again deals mostly with housekeeping issues would be a disaster at this moment in our history. Much of the normal agenda must be put aside in order to give full attention to what is truly important. General Synod members need to come determined to get to the root of our problems no matter what. The Church has many very gifted people working for it as well as abundant resources to which it has access. The various Committees of the Synod can bend themselves to the same task. We cannot afford to go blindly into the dark.

3) Establish Our Core Doctrine

Thirdly, it is absolutely critical that this General Synod commit the Church to a process designed to end the ambiguity and confusion over the "doctrine of the Anglican Church of Canada". The basic Christian beliefs and principles which we supposedly hold in common must be re-articulated and carefully defined if they are to have any meaning at all. Not only must we discover what these are, we must commit ourselves, as a whole Church, to believe, uphold, teach, defend, and live these beliefs. We must be absolutely clear about what we really do believe and what the range of acceptable interpretation might be.

Part of the task will be to articulate and commit ourselves to the genuine Anglican position on the nature and authority of Holy Scripture. As I pointed out earlier in this work ("Underneath The Bible", p. 48ff.), an implicit understanding of these truths underlays not only the doctrinal structure of Anglicanism but also of the church universal. This unspoken assumption now needs to be made explicit. This follows in the pattern of the early church which often was forced to articulate its implicit faith in the face of erroneous teaching. It has fallen to our generation to deal with the doctrine of Scripture. The fact that this has not been part of our tradition simply means that we have not had to deal with it until now. We are at one of those pivotal moments in the life of the Church. It is exciting and frightening at the same time!

Once we have re-discovered our common beliefs we will find ourselves in a position to deal positively and faithfully with the whole range of questions that confront contemporary Anglicans, including homosexuality. More importantly, we will also be able to come to a shared understanding of our mission in the modern world and get on with the task. This is, after all, our reason to exist. A common agenda can only arise out of a common faith.

(c) Conclusion: "Carpe Diem!"

In the earlier part of this book I spoke a lot about the fragmentization of our Church and the destructive, demoralizing effect it has had. We now have what I believe may be a God-given opportunity to reverse this process, pick up the pieces and put them back together again. We are unlikely to get another chance. This is the moment. "Carpe diem!", as the ancient Romans used to say: "Seize the day!"

CHAPTER EIGHT

Speaking With One V.O.I.C.E.

And do this, understanding the present time. The hour has come for you to wake from your slumber, because our salvation is nearer now than when we first believed. The night is nearly over; the day is almost here.
(Romans 13:11-12a)

(i) Asking the Right Question

The previous chapter indicated that the pressing crisis in the Anglican Church of Canada actually presents it with an extraordinary opportunity for reform and renewal. It will be recalled that in order to take advantage of this opportunity it will be necessary for this coming General Synod to address this crisis with unblinking resolve.

The problem is that past General Synods have given little indication that they were seriously interested in dealing with the true situation. While there is a variety of reasons for this, *the bottom line is that most of the members of Synod felt insufficient urgency to overcome their natural reluctance, delve beneath the surface of things, bring the crisis out into the open and deal with it.* Although the sense of urgency should be greater in 1998, especially with some bishops hinting at the eventual possibility of schism over the issue of homosexuality (p. 113), there is as yet scant evidence that delegates will be interested in taking this critical step.

The question then becomes, "How can the members of the coming General Synod acquire a greater sense of urgency about the crisis in the

Church?", knowing that only this will motivate them to help get things moving away from the edge of the abyss and toward resolution.

There is an answer to this question. It arises out of an understanding of some important aspects of the nature and structure of General Synod.

(ii) Looking Right Into It

The Canadian Anglican Church is made up of thirty dioceses, each of which, at its own Synod, elects its delegates to the General Synod. Using a formula based on the number of ordained persons in the diocese they choose their quota of lay and clergy representatives. This usually takes place about a year before the national body convenes. It does this every three years in a different part of the country. Although those elected are officially called "members" of General Synod, they are commonly seen as "delegates" whose task it is to represent their diocese at the National level. Bishops and other officials are automatically part of General Synod.

Together there are three "houses" that make up General Synod: laity, clergy and bishops. In 1995 there was a total of about 300 members, with diocesan representation ranging from Toronto with twenty-four members to Yukon with four. Some measures, and it is likely that any resolutions aimed at dealing directly with our crisis would be included among them, need a majority in each "house" in order to pass (as opposed to a simple majority of all members present). Any attempt to deal with General Synod members outside of the normal electoral process (for which there is now neither time nor easy access) needs to keep these facts in mind.

Since the identities of most of the three-hundred plus members of General Synod are known at least one year in advance it is theoretically possible for ordinary parishioners to communicate their concerns directly to their diocesan delegates. However, because delegates are chosen at a level one step removed from the grassroots, this is very rarely done. Most parishioners seem neither to know who their representatives are nor that they even have such representatives! Their names and addresses are, however, readily available from the various diocesan offices. There is nothing to stop Church members from letting their General Synod delegates know how they feel about the various issues facing the Church. Many delegates would no doubt welcome such input because they too sense their isolation from those in the pew.

When we add to these considerations the fact that the theme for the 1998 Synod is "Lift Every Voice", a plan of action suggests itself. It is a plan which has the potential of enabling literally every voice in the Church to be lifted.

(iii) Doing the Write Thing

What if each member of General Synod was to receive several hundred (thousand?) letters from concerned parishes and individuals in their diocese urging them to 1) support the recent stand of the bishops against the ordination of practicing homosexuals and the blessing of same-sex unions; 2) give their full attention to the crisis in the Church and 3) initiate a process whereby the basic Christian beliefs of the Anglican Church of Canada could be effectively articulated and re-affirmed?

Would not such an unprecedented action have a tremendous effect?

It would certainly let the delegates know for sure that: 1) large numbers of Anglicans are deeply opposed to the acceptance of practicing homosexuality; 2) there is widespread and grave concern among its members over the overall crisis in the Church and they want to see it addressed in a direct and positive manner; 3) there is a broadly shared perception that our Church is unsure of what it believes anymore and that this confusion must be cleared up and basic Christian doctrine affirmed before we can have any secure hope in denominational recovery; 4) there is a large scale sense of urgency about these matters and that this coming Synod can ill afford to carry on business as usual.

It would greatly encourage those members of General Synod who already share these concerns to take action. We must not imagine that Synod delegates have been totally unaware of the gathering crisis in the Church. They are, if anything, more aware of the real situation than the rest of us. What they seem to have lacked is enough motivation to overcome the inertia and reluctance that is normal when we are faced with problems that just seem too big for us. Most of us would exactly the same way. Receiving a deluge of support for specific action from throughout their own dioceses would inspire and direct delegates in their efforts on the floor of the Synod.

It would also mean that the leadership which the last Synod seemed to pass on to the local level would take on an unexpected but powerful reality. The 1995 restructuring of General Synod according to the Strategic Plan passed on a number of responsibilities to the grassroots. Many at this level have felt powerless in their distress over the direction the Church seems to have been going. By expressing their concern directly to their members of General Synod, they will have accepted the challenge of the Synod itself and become involved. Ironically, their involvement would strongly remind General Synod of its own responsibilities, as the central leadership of the Church, to deal with matters of central concern to the whole body. Only their level can effectively address the critical issue of a fundamentally divided denomination. This cannot be passed down to lower levels.

What I am describing, I realize, would amount to nothing short of a revolution. The people have the power. They can "lift every voice" and make a profound difference in the direction taken by the Anglican Church of Canada. The time for them to act is now! The future of the denomination lies in their hands, their writing hands. If they will take this action then there is truly hope. If they do not, if there is little support for the agenda I have outlined above, then I fear for the future. If we have one.

(iv) Writing the Right Letter

Ideally each Anglican who is moved to inform his or her delegates will sit down and compose a short letter outlining their concerns. This letter should be articulate and to the point. In addition, it must include a clear statement of personal support for the kind of action that I have suggested. Delegates must be urged to support those motions which support the taking of serious action on our true crisis when they are introduced onto the floor of General Synod. Of course this means that each one who is writing such a letter would have to send it to *each* diocesan delegate (including the bishop) and perhaps the Primate as well. The names and addresses of these persons would have to be obtained from the local diocesan office, from diocesan synod delegates or from parish priests.

This is quite a lot to expect from a people who are not used to taking this kind of action. No wonder I said "ideally" at the beginning of the last paragraph! In fact, after long consideration of the matter I have come to the conclusion that it is in fact too much to expect. The process needs significant simplification.

Because something must be done, I have helped create an organization called V.O.I.C.E. (Vocalizing Our Interest in Church Endeavours) in order to make the job as easy as possible. Here is what it is set up to do:

1) In Appendix D to this book will be found a fold-out (and reproducible) "form letter" which we offer to all those who wish to stand up and be counted but would prefer not to send the personal letter suggested above.

2) If this letter is completed and returned to V.O.I.C.E. at the address provided, we will undertake to make sure that a copy is sent to each of the respondent's delegates to General Synod, the appropriate diocesan bishop and the Primate. Each of the letters must be signed and give the address and diocese of the person writing.

3) Persons sending a fully personal letter may also send it to V.O.I.C.E. and we will ensure that it is copied and sent out to the appropriate members of General Synod.

4) V.O.I.C.E. will also keep a copy on file so that we can issue a report to the whole church sometime before the upcoming General Synod as to how many of these responses we have received. Even those who write directly to their delegates should send a copy to V.O.I.C.E. in order to keep as accurate a count as possible.

5) Although it is possible for large numbers of persons to sign one of the form letters in a kind of petition, it is strongly recommended that this be avoided. Individual letters will have much more effect.

6) Parish Corporations, Vestries and Councils, Deaneries, Diocesan Councils, ACW groups and any other "official" bodies of the ACC are also encouraged to write. Of course it must be understood that this should not replace the need of each individual member to write as well.

7) V.O.I.C.E. will not involve itself in forwarding letters that express hatred, accusations, anger or any other unchristian attitudes. Any such letters received will be returned to the sender with an explanation.

In a country the size of Canada it is essential to have an organized centre to give proper focus to any national effort. It may well be that similar efforts are underway in other parts of Canada but not yet visible on the national scene. V.O.I.C.E. will cooperate with others working to the same end. In any event, anyone who wishes to participate in the V.O.I.C.E. campaign only has to take a few moments to fill in the form and mail it to one address. What could be simpler?

It may be simple but it is not easy or without spiritual risk. I recognize that many today are reluctant to speak up on these matters because of the fear of being labeled "homophobic". While we must not let this fear hold us back, we must nevertheless listen carefully to what lies behind this accusation. Homophobia, as a very real irrational hatred and loathing of homosexuals, has indeed motivated many of the verbal and physical attacks that homosexual persons have suffered. Understandably, for many homosexuals (and others), such hatred lies at the root of *all* opposition to their lifestyle. *As Christians, we must repent of all such hatred and closely examine our motives in taking our stand.* Is it truly out of love for the homosexual as well as for Christ and his church that we express our concern? Our opposition to the practice of homosexuality must be always be a principled opposition, concerned with both truth and justice. We must make it crystal clear that our overriding concern is not with homosexuality but with the real problem: the fact that we have two religions in the same Church. When we speak from this perspective we have the right to be heard. Please God that this will be the case with all those who dare to take action in the present crisis.

(v) Writing the Right Book

I, for one, have decided to write. Hence this book.

I wanted to tell the truth as best I could. *In the hope that the truth carries its own conviction I have undertaken to send a copy of this book to all three hundred or so members of the 1998 General Synod.* In my mind the evidence is irrefutable: the Anglican Church is in serious crisis because it has two religions in the same institution and one of them, liberalism, is in deadly opposition to the traditional/orthodox faith of our heritage. Perhaps if members of Synod read this book it can help make a difference. Some may find in it an articulation of their own feelings. Others may even come to share in my conclusions. I hope that those who remain unconvinced might come at least to agree that the argument has merit and deserves a thorough investigation. The stakes are extremely high, after all.

However, it is one thing to know the truth and quite another to act and to act appropriately on that knowledge. After all, many in the Church leadership are already well-acquainted with the truth but have not yet taken official action to deal with it. That is where the V.O.I.C.E. letter writing campaign comes in and why it and any similar initiatives are critically important. They will help spur the Synod on to action.

Of course the letters will not get written at all if ordinary Anglicans remain uninformed about the situation that their Church is truly in and about what they can do about it. Again, this is a major reason for my writing. My hope is to encourage hundreds, perhaps even thousands, of these "ordinary Anglicans" to do what they can do to help save their Church. Maybe if they do the "write" thing the rest of us might do the "right" thing too.

Perhaps I am just a V.O.I.C.E. crying out in the wilderness.

Am I?

(vi) Reality Check: A Letter From the Abyss

One thing is certain. If the so-called "silent majority" remain silent, if they do not get involved, then they will share the blame for the consequences. I have already argued earlier that we can expect to see events unfold in the Anglican Church in ways that parallel what happened in the United Church of Canada. Recently all of Canada has become aware that the current moderator of that Church, the Very Reverend Bill Phipps, flatly denies the basic doctrines of the historic Christian faith. He has openly proclaimed that he cannot accept that Jesus is God or that he rose bodily from the dead, among other things. By now this should come as no surprise to my readers but it is still shocking. This is only because Rev. Phipps is just being more forthright than his predecessors. His opinions are quite unremarkable for a minister in any mainline denomination, including the Anglican Church of Canada. Such theories have been taught and caught in most of our theological colleges for years.

Homosexuality was the watershed issue for the United Church. Beyond this marker there was no turning back. Now members are learning the full truth: the leaders who ushered them into this new age had already abandoned the traditional/orthodox faith upon which their Church was founded. Anne Squires, who was the moderator during that Church's crisis over the ordination of practicing homosexuals now tells us that she too rejects the traditional interpretation of the Scriptures. According to a recent report in *The Globe and Mail* (Nov. 15, 1997) she prefers to believe that the Gospel writers used the language of mythology and story to convey the basic truths about Jesus and his ministry. Regarding the continuing controversy regarding these matters she says, "Our ministers are to blame because they tend not to teach the congregation what they themselves have learned in theological college. They don't want to stir up a lot of debate and discussion."

Here is the living proof of my thesis that the real issue is not homosexuality but the widespread acceptance of the new religion of liberalism. *This* is the disease. The push to accept practicing homosexuality is *only the symptom*. But it cannot be ignored. We Anglicans, faced now with the same symptom, still have a briefly opened window of opportunity to make a difference by writing our General Synod delegates.

If we don't act now we will no doubt be writing another kind of letter in the future. It may be similar to this one which appeared recently in the Saint John (New Brunswick) *Times-Globe* shortly after a local United Church minister officiated at a "covenanting service" between two gay men. There was an outpouring of intense opposition to this from many local members of that denomination. *This letter was written to remind such persons that they had had their opportunity to do something about this situation but they had not taken it.*

> As a life member of the United Church of Canada I would like to express my views on the events leading up to the present situation in the Church.
>
> Why all the hubbub concerning the same-sex marriage in one of our city churches? Didn't United Church members see it coming? Wasn't the writing on the wall? Where were the congregations years ago when General Council was considering ordaining ministers regardless of their sexual orientation? Where were the crowds when meetings were held to oppose this matter? Did the clergy properly inform their congregations as to what was happening?
>
> People said it would never happen, that they didn't want to talk about it. But it did happen, didn't it? Why did Christian delegates to General Council support it, many claiming they were harassed by small minorities? Are they sorry today or are they glad they accepted it? Why was one very concerned minister who fought hard in his Presbytery and at Victoria (where the fateful General Council was held) not supported?
>
> We, the United Church members, let it happen. We must all bear the blame. Perhaps we should be more familiar with the Scriptures.
>
> Why haven't we joined the Community of Concern, a body of people extremely concerned about where our church is heading and the changes that have been made? Are we going to accept other changes? Or will this issue be a lesson to us that we must all fight? For if we had in the beginning, this would never have happened. I pray that our church will survive the many generations to come, if not for ourselves, for our children and their children's children.
>
> B.F.,
> Saint John, N.B.

This is a very sad letter. It is a letter from the abyss. Is it also a letter from our future?

Only time will tell.

CHAPTER NINE

What More Can I Do?

"I have become all things to all men that by all possible means I might save some."(1 Corinthians 9:22a)

Although it is absolutely critical that every concerned Anglican communicate his opinion to his General Synod delegates, this is not all that needs to be done. This chapter will draw a few other needful things to my readers' attention. I hope that we will avail ourselves of "all possible means" as we press on toward the goal.

(i) Pray

First of all, there is the matter of prayer. We must commit ourselves to pray regularly for the Church.. This includes the General Synod of May 1998, meeting in Montreal. Our leaders are going to need the wisdom of Solomon as they deal with an unprecedented situation. By virtue of their office they deserve our respect and support and even when we are driven to the conclusion that some have decided to worship another god, they should be treated with grace and dignity. This will strain many of us to the breaking point compelling us to pray for humility, wisdom, courage and grace. A united effort is needed to save the Church and this, alas, has often exceeded our grasp.

Nothing that we can do will succeed without the undergirding of prayer. This is spiritual warfare and we need to use spiritual weapons, not against people but against principalities and powers, against the world, the flesh and the devil. Even if we win, we could lose, caught up in triumphalism and pride. Though hard to accept, it may be God's purpose to allow the Anglican Church of Canada to slide into the abyss. Perhaps this is his judgement upon us. We must be truly open to his will and not our own. This can only come as we submit ourselves to him in prayer (and, might I suggest, some fasting too!). Whatever action we decide to take should arise out of deliberate prayer. John Sperry, retired Bishop of The Arctic, has recently composed an excellent prayer for the Church and it is included as Appendix B at the end of this book.

(ii) Ask the Bishops Where They Stand

In the Anglican system it is the bishops, as shepherds of the flock, who have primary leadership responsibility. They are the guardians and teachers of "the faith once delivered to the saints". As was noted in Chapter Two (see "The Silence of the Shepherds", p. 36) they have remained largely silent on the fact that the denomination is in serious crisis. Nor have they addressed the true nature of the crisis, at least in public.

Surely it is time for them to break the silence and level with us. What is going on? With the recent public "vote" on the issue of the ordination of practicing homosexuals their own confusion and division is evident. We still do not know what exactly they believe about this issue or the others that the Church is dealing with (such as goddess worship, evangelism, the fragmentization of the Church, mission etc.)? Are they prepared to affirm unequivocally and personally the received doctrine of the Church? If not, how do they justify their position as leaders of that Church? We want to know. We need to know. We deserve to know. If the bishops are not accountable to the Church, to whom are they accountable? We Anglicans should be requesting our bishops to tell us clearly where they stand, not as politicians who need to fear reelection but as the chief pastors of a very confused flock. Where are they prepared to take us? Ask them. And keep on asking until a clear answer is given.

This asking must be done with respect for the great office of bishop. It must be done out of genuine concern for the man or woman in that office. There is no room for malice or invective. Be firm but be polite. This is only asking them to be honest with us and to assume their role as shepherds of the flock and guardians of the truth. And pray for them. They bear great burdens and face momentous decisions.

(iii) Support Those Already On Their Feet

I realize that I may have left the impression that our entire leadership has been seriously compromised by the advent of liberalism. This is not true. But, while *all* of us have been influenced to some degree by the liberal way of thinking, it does seem to predominate at the higher levels in the Church. It is all the more important, then, to support those among them that do stand up to be counted. Whenever we see a bishop or anyone in leadership proclaiming the truth of traditional/orthodox Christianity we should let them know that they are appreciated, that they do not stand alone.

When most of the parish of St. Alban's in Port Alberni, BC, voted to leave its diocese for reasons with which many Anglicans could identify, the Primate dismissed this action as an isolated event (suggesting that the action of St. Alban's had no more implication than that "one parish is unhappy with the actions of General Synod" and that such opposition to the official agenda is restricted to "a small group of people from one part of the country."). Every Anglican who is in basic sympathy with the stand the parish has taken and shares in the same frustration with the current state of the Church should write to the rector of that congregation, sending a copy to the Primate, to his or her own bishop and to the bishop of British Columbia in Victoria. Think of how lonely those people must now feel out there in the silence, our silence. Think of how our leaders need to know how many of us feel about what happened. Further opportunities to lend support will present themselves as individuals, bishops, rectors, scholars, parishes, groups of parishes, organizations and even dioceses begin to get to their feet. Let us all stand together!

(iv) Give to the Cause

Those organizations within our ranks which seek to uphold and minister out of the traditional/orthodox Christian faith also need to be supported. For those who wish to aid biblically focused mission activity there is the South American Missionary Society. For those who desire evangelistic missions and outreach there is the Church Army. For those who would like to deepen the life of prayer there is the Anglican Fellowship of Prayer. For those interested in strengthening the family there is the Mothers' Union. Beyond these special interest groups (and there are others), are three organizations that are working specifically for the biblical renewal of the ACC, each coming at the task from its own perspective. These are the Prayer Book Society of Canada (traditionalist), the Anglican Renewal Movement (charismatic) and Barnabas Anglican Ministries (evangelical). Membership in these groups is not mutually exclusive but they have tended not to work together. Until recently. And that is one of the most hopeful and important developments in our history.

Seeing the need for all traditional/orthodox Anglicans to come together in this time of crisis (always, unfortunately, an excellent motive for co-operation) these three associations sponsored Essentials 94. This was a conference held on the island of Montreal in June of 1994 in order to try to address the perceived drift of our Church away from the basic truths of the Christian faith. While the organizers hoped for 400, more than 700 Anglicans attended including six of our current bishops. It gave tremendous encouragement to those present from all across Canada. It was a miracle! People went home excited about the possibilities of renewal and as a result there have been a large number of follow-up conferences and events right across the country. Some have had as many as 500 in attendance while others might have only 30 or 40. All have been lively. In addition to these results, Essentials 94 issued "*The Montreal Declaration of Anglican Essentials*" which articulated fifteen "essentials" of the traditional/orthodox faith in a contemporary Canadian Anglican context. Not content with this, Essentials 94 went on to publish all the papers that were presented at the conference in a book entitled *Anglican Essentials: Reclaiming Faith in the Anglican Church of Canada* (George Egerton, ed.). Essentials 94 has spawned something of a movement. It has become simply "Essentials" and is now governed by the Essentials Council.

This is the time to offer these organizations, especially Essentials as the umbrella group, all the support we can. Each of them operates on a shoe-string budget. They do not have the taxing power of the official Church structures and so are constantly in need of finances. Most of their current supporters are highly committed persons who give generously to their local parishes and find it difficult to extend themselves much further. The situation is critical, however. I would ask every Anglican who sympathizes with these groups to make an extraordinary effort to dig deep in order to keep them alive and well over the next five years. Their continued presence can greatly influence the shape of the coming Church. At present their efforts are crippled by a lack of funds and this is just the time they should be freed up to do all that is possible. Appendix A contains the names and addresses of these organizations and their publications. Let's do it!

(v) Encourage the *Anglican Journal*

Essentials 94 was undoubtedly one of the most important events in the history of our denomination and yet it has received relatively little coverage in the *Anglican Journal*. It has been very difficult, as an "unofficial" body in the Church, to get the attention of the denominational newspaper. The fact that many of us are coming together in significant numbers for on-going Essentials events is an unprecedented development. Of course the Journal is in a difficult position because if it gives greater coverage to Essentials (or, for example, to the splendid work of the South American Missionary Society or to the maturing vision of the Prayer Book Society) it may not sit well with the "official" Church. Under the circumstances, Essentials and its sympathizers should be thankful for the coverage they have received. Certainly it has helped provoke a liberal critique of Essentials and this has gone a long way to breaking the silence. It would be gratifying to see the *Journal* really dig into this story, find out what is really happening in the Church and fully inform its readers. A few thousand letters to the editor might have some effect on the situation. By the way, the editor, David Harris, should be commended for some of the efforts he has been making. He has clearly felt some of the tremors and is wondering out loud what they mean.

(vi) Push This Book

At the small risk of being accused of beating my own drum might I suggest that, if this book has been helpful to anyone, efforts be made to ensure its wide dissemination. As a self-published book it does not have ready access to the usual means of distribution. It needs to be reviewed in diocesan papers, mentioned in letters to the editor, put into local bookstores. Perhaps it could be purchased in quantity and given away. It could be used for parish study or sermon material. The object is to make sure that everyone who *should* read it *does* read it. All of the royalties (if any!) will be going towards the ongoing work of the biblical reformation of the Anglican Church of Canada.

(vii) Get Involved in the Structures of the Church

For the longer term there is no doubt that it would be possible to effect considerable change through denominational structures that are already in place. For all the feeling of exclusion that many traditional/orthodox Anglicans seem to feel, these structures are in several ways very open to their involvement. However, in order to take full advantage of this fact a few critical adjustments would need to be made.

In many ways much of the power within the Anglican Church of Canada is in the hands of the people and most of it is centred within the synodical form of government. At their Annual Meetings parishes elect delegates to their diocesan synod and many of the important decisions are made here, up to and including the election of a new bishop. The members of diocesan synods also choose from their number delegates to the General Synod where decisions are made for the entire denomination.

This looks like a normal democratic system but the fear of the "party spirit" has kept the politicking strictly to the back room. This means that when delegates to synod are chosen, unless you know the candidate personally, there is no way to determine what their positions are on the various issues that face the Church. At the parish level this is less of an issue. The problem there is often just trying to find someone who will volunteer to go. Parishes need to put a greater priority on these elections. At the diocesan synod delegates are in a room full of strangers. When asked to choose, say, eight of them for General Synod, there is often only table gossip to rely upon for any information about the candidates. It is a bit of a farce to conduct elections in this fashion. We just don't know who we are voting for. Those elected seem often to be those who tend to "go to the microphones" the most with their opinions. In this forum that is perhaps the only way to be able to identify someone at election time.

In spite of these limitations it still is a democratic process and therefore open to all members of the Church to get involved and make a difference. True, you need to be a bit of a political animal, one who enjoys the rough and tumble of debate, stands up for what he believes, is willing to listen to silly arguments and pays attention to boring details in reports etc.

Besides running for elected offices in the Church there is always a place for volunteers, especially on the myriads of committees which seem to be a necessary part of our denominational life. Again it takes a special kind of person to do this kind of work. For those so inclined it can be a very important role to play in bringing about reform and renewal. It takes time and patience but it can work.

(viii) Will They Come?

I am reminded of the movie "Field of Dreams" which starred Kevin Costner. As the central character, Costner played a baseball fan who heard a voice tell him to build a baseball field out in the middle of the Kansas prairie. The voice also said, "If you build it, they will come." The "they" in question were the ghosts of legendary heroes of baseball such as Ty Cobb and Babe Ruth. Being a bit of a dreamer he constructed the field and then waited. Would they come? Or would he be proved a fool?

I identify with Costner's character. With this book and the creation of V.O.I.C.E. I have provided a structure which others might be able to use for a great purpose. Is this just a "field of dreams"?

Or will they come?

CHAPTER TEN

Just Imagine!

I saw the Holy City, the new Jerusalem, coming down out of heaven from God, prepared as a bride beautifully dressed for her husband, And I heard a loud voice from the throne saying, "Now the dwelling of God is with men, and he will live with them. They will be his people, and God himself will be with them and be their God. He will wipe every tear from their eyes. There will be no more death or mourning or crying or pain, for the old order of things has passed away." (Revelation 21:2-4)

My readers may be excused if they have gotten the impression that my only purpose in writing this book was to help prevent the Anglican Church of Canada from committing an act of self-destruction. I hope that many would agree that this is a worthwhile goal in and of itself.

But it is not enough. We must be inspired by a greater and more positive vision: a vision of the Church restored, reformed and renewed. Such a vision must begin with an act of the imagination.

So, imagine.

Imagine a Church agreeing in the truth of God's holy Word, and living in unity and godly love. Imagine a Church able to articulate a saving message to a confused and wayward nation. Imagine a Church whose leadership speaks with one voice representing us all. Imagine a Church sure of its way in a darkening age, drawing on the wisdom of the ages but open to engage new realities with God's truth. Imagine a Church at peace with itself. Imagine a Church of rich diversity centred in the essentials of the catholic faith. Imagine a Church whose seminaries and scholars explore and defend the faith once delivered to the saints. Imagine a Church whose synods and committees readily attracted the brightest and the best. Imagine a Church mobilized for ministry and focussed upon one common mission. Imagine a Church in which the laity were full partners in the Gospel, learning, living and sharing the faith. Imagine a Church whose clergy are in fundamental agreement with one another, able to work together across parish lines. Imagine a Church which is full of energy, willing and able to get on with the great task entrusted to it by the Lord Jesus himself. Imagine a Church at common prayer together. Imagine a Church which has returned to its first love. Imagine a Church that has been made whole again, no longer rent asunder by two religions. Imagine!

This, surely, must be our sustaining vision. It is also, thank God, the promise that lies at the heart of the current crisis. While our situation is terribly difficult to face, it has at the same time the awesome potential of providing Anglicans with an incentive to stand up at last and be counted. And if they do, the Church will be presented with an unprecedented opportunity for a return to vitality and purpose. Imagine!

Just imagine.

He said to me: "It is done. I am the Alpha and the Omega, the Beginning and the End. To him who is thirsty I will give to drink without cost from the spring of the water of life. He who overcomes will inherit all this...."
(Revelation 6-7a)

I Have Made My Point

Is division our destiny?

Let there be no mistake. We have two religions in one Church. There are only two possible resolutions to this dilemma.

We can become two separate but weakened Churches, each with its own religion. Presently, the two religions are on a collision course over the issue of practicing homosexuality. This will lead inevitably to the abyss of open schism as the fundamental division presently beneath the surface erupts into the open.

Or we can become one Church with one religion. This is the path I am urging us to take. It is the hard path of repentance and conversion, of rejection of liberalism and recommitment to the traditional/orthodox Christianity of our heritage. Like all conversions, it will only be accomplished as we are moved by the Holy Spirit. It will require much persuasion and grace. And time.

Thanks to the House of Bishops we have
some time in which to act. It is critical
breathing space during which we must turn
our attention away from the homosexual
issue and toward the real problem.

Otherwise, division *is* our destiny.

We cannot stand idly by.

Can we?

APPENDIX A

TRADITIONAL/ORTHODOX ORGANIZATIONS AND PUBLICATIONS

1) Charismatic: Anglican Renewal Ministries
8 Withrow Ave.,
Nepean, ON, K2G 2H6

Publication: *Anglicans for Renewal Canada*

2) Evangelical: Barnabas Anglican Ministries
1749 Argyle St.,
Halifax, NS, B3J 3K4

Publication: *INCOURAGE*

3) Traditional: The Prayer Book Society of Canada
P.O. Box 38060
1430 Prince of Wales Dr.
Ottawa, ON, K2C 3Y7

Publications: *NEWSLETTER*
The Machray Review

4) Coalition of above three: Essentials
Box 414,
Halifax, NS, B3J 2P8

Publications: *Montreal Declaration of Anglican Essentials*
Anglican Essentials: Reclaiming Faith in the Anglican Church of Canada
Anglican Essentials Study Guide
Dr. J.I. Packer's Commentary on the Montreal Declaration

6) Evangelism and Social Ministry: The Church Army in Canada
397 Brunswick Ave.,
Toronto, ON, M5R 2Z2

Publication : *The Crusader*

7) Missions: The South American Missionary Society
P.O. Box 26043,
Barrie, ON, L4N 7N3

Publication: SAMS *News*

8) Theological Education: Wycliffe College
5 Hoskin Ave.,
Toronto, ON, M5S 1H2

9) To Contact Former Parishioners and Rector of St. Alban's, Port Alberni,

Please Write: The Rev. John Cox
Alberni Christian Fellowship
4006 - 8th Ave.,
Port Alberni, BC, V9T 4S4

APPENDIX B

"A PRAYER FOR THE CHURCH"

Almighty God and Father of our Lord Jesus Christ: coming into our world in the person of your Son through his redemptive self-offering, you have called us into a new relationship as your sons and daughters in the family of your One, Holy, Apostolic Church.

We offer our thanksgiving that by the power of the Holy Spirit, the Church, as created and expressed among us, has been sustained over so many centuries: we pray that we, in this our own generation, may remain faithful to its life and witness as revealed in your holy Word.

In penitence, and in your presence, we acknowledge our sin:-

> **.....for far too often desiring to recreate you more in our own image as against the humble acceptance that, despite the defacing by sin, we have been created in yours for lives that reflect your glory.**
>
> **.....for our readiness to re-interpret holy Scripture more to accommodate the inclinations of our liberal society as against the upholding of revealed standards of**

human behaviour declared so forcibly in your Word.

.....for exchanging the conviction of our forbears that the Lord Jesus Christ in his personhood and redemptive mission is unique, amid current pressures to relegate him as a valid focus of faith together with the gods, sages and prophets of other contemporary faiths.

.....for exchanging the divine proclamation that in Christ, the broken condition of human beings through sin in all its forms, body, soul and spirit, is an authentic subject for healing and renewal as against selective causes for celebration.

Lord, in your mercy, create among us a renewed commitment to the Church as brought into life 'by the blood of the everlasting covenant' through the power of the Holy Spirit.

'Fill your Church with all truth: in all truth with all peace. Where it is corrupt, purify it; where it is in error, direct it; where anything is amiss, reform it; where it is right, strengthen and confirm it; where it is in want, furnish it; where it is divided and rent asunder, make it whole again; through Jesus Christ our Lord.'

Amen.

Bishop John Sperry
December 1996

(Used by Permission of the Author)

APPENDIX C

INSUFFICIENT OBJECTIONS

The Following Statements Are Sometimes Directed At Efforts to Have the Church Articulate and Affirm its Central Doctrines. Each Is Followed By a "Response" indicating a reason or two for its inadequacy.

1. "Ours is not a 'Confessional' Church. We have never required adherence to a 'Confession of Faith'."

> Response: This has some truth to it, if you ignore the Apostles' and Nicene Creeds which are to be accepted by all Anglicans. Perhaps, as well, this lack of a Confession of Faith" is one of our traditions which needs discarding in this modern era. Surely we should not be maintaining an antiquated tradition.

2. "Those in positions of leadership should publicly support the official positions of the Church but may privately differ with them".

> Response: What is the difference between this and hypocrisy? How can a Christian say he or she believes one thing in public and another in private? Where is the integrity in this?

3. "All of our leaders are sworn to uphold the "doctrine of the Anglican Church of Canada".

> Response: Until the "doctrine of the Anglican Church of Canada" is defined, and carefully defined, this statement is meaningless. So also are all statements that suggest that such

doctrine is unchangeable, enjoying some type of existence beyond the reach of time and space.

4. "I am opposed to any group within the Church trying to tell the rest of us what to believe."

Response: Exactly. That is why General Synod must take on this task. At the same time one must wonder why there is so much objection to, say, *The Montreal Declaration of Anglican Essentials,* when all that document did, more or less, was reaffirm the basic beliefs of catholic Christianity. What's the problem?

5. "Doctrinal matters are always subject to various interpretations."

Response: This is true to some extent. Yet there must be a central core of beliefs that we hold in common if we are to continue to exist as a functioning Church. If we cannot agree to "the Anglican interpretation" of these doctrines then we have no reason to hope for a common future.

6. "I don't think that I should force my belief or my interpretation upon anyone else."

Response: No one is suggesting such a thing. It is just that one Church cannot contain an infinite number of views and still continue to function. Its members need to have a shared understanding of its core beliefs. It should be a voluntary association of like-minded (to a degree) persons committed to the same goals. Others who do not share in these convictions are free to form their own association around whatever it is they believe.

7. "We are all Anglicans together. Let us just put aside our differences and get on with the job."

Response: This is a very seductive statement but it hides a number of false assumptions. In what sense are we "together"? Is it possible to "get on with the job" when we differ deeply about what that job is? Are these "differences" mere trifles which can be "put aside" or do they go to the core of who we are as Christian people?

8. "I abhor the idea of having "thought police" in the Anglican Church."

Response: Again, nobody is suggesting this. The insistence on a personal commitment to the central doctrines of one's Church seems like a simple enough thing to do. Why is it resisted with such fervour? We already go through a *form* of this commitment. Why not give it real integrity and meaning?

9. "I honestly don't see what the problem is."

Response: Read this book.

A NOTE REGARDING FINANCES

It is expected that the cost of the V.O.I.C.E. campaign will be recovered from the revenues generated by the sale of this book. DONATIONS, however, would be welcome in order to ensure that no debts are incurred. V.O.I.C.E. is NOT a Registered Charity for Income Tax purposes. If you desire an Income Tax Receipt, please make your cheque payable to "St. John's (Stone) Church" and mark it clearly as a donation for V.O.I.C.E. ***Thank you.***

V.O.I.C.E.
87 Carleton St.,
Saint John, NB
E2L 2Z2

CALL Toll-Free
1-800-456-3030

PHONE: 642- 5658

FAX: 506-642-5899